Dancing Along the Deadline

Ezra Hoyt Ripple, circa 1905

The Andersonville Memoir of a
Prisoner of the Confederacy

Dancing Along the Deadline

Ezra Hoyt Ripple
Edited by Mark A. Snell

PRESIDIO

Published by Presidio Press
505 B San Marin Dr., Suite 300
Novato, CA 94945-1340

Library of Congress Cataloging-in-Publication Data

ISBN 0-89141-577-7 (hardcover)

Illustrations courtesy Susan Hinkel

Printed in the United States of America

Contents

Foreword

"Denied a soldier's splendid death/Where glory rolls her martial drum/They tasted death at every breath/And bravely met their martyrdom."[1] So goes a verse of the poem inscribed on one of the bronze tablets adorning the Pennsylvania Memorial in Andersonville National Cemetery. Dedicated on December 7, 1905, the monument was authorized by an act of the Pennsylvania legislature to "commemorate the heroism, sacrifices and patriotism of the Pennsylvania soldiers in the Union Armies . . . who died at Andersonville Prison, Georgia, while confined there as prisoners of war." On another tablet the names of the members of the Pennsylvania Andersonville Memorial Commission are recorded. Among the men listed was the author of these memoirs, Ezra H. Ripple, who was appointed by Governor William A. Stone on October 15, 1901, to serve as the "Secretary & Treasurer of the Commission."[2] Almost four decades earlier, as a private in Company K, 52nd Pennsylvania Volunteer Infantry Regiment, Ripple was captured on July 3, 1864 during his regiment's attempt to take and hold James Island in Charleston Harbor, South Carolina. Private Ripple spent the next nine months as a prisoner of the Confederate States of America at the notorious Andersonville Prison and later at the Florence (South Carolina) Prison.

Ezra Hoyt Ripple was born on February 14, 1842, in Mauch Chunk, a small town in northeastern Pennsylvania. Ezra was one of Silas and Elizabeth Ripple's three children, of which only two reached adulthood. When Ezra was four years old his parents moved to Buck Mountain, Pennsylvania, where he attended the common schools and where he later completed his education at Wyoming Seminary in 1857. That year the Ripple family moved to Scranton, where Ezra assisted Silas in his new career as a hotel proprietor. Upon Silas Ripple's death, Ezra became a druggist, an endeavor he continued until his enlistment in the 52nd Pennsylvania on March 24, 1864. By then, the black-eyed, brown-haired Ripple had served two short stints in Pennsylvania "emergency" regiments that had been raised to help counter the Army of Northern Virginia's two invasions of the North.[3]

The 52nd Pennsylvania was formed in July 1861 in response to President Lincoln's call to the loyal states for three-year regiments. Recruited primarily from the northeastern Pennsylvania counties of Wyoming, Clinton, Bradford, Union, Luzerne, and Schuykill, the 52nd participated in the Peninsula Campaign as part of Major General Erasmus D. Keyes's Fourth Corps, Army of the Potomac. During what proved to be a bloody series of engagements for the 52nd, the regiment's historian proudly noted that "no other regiment encamped so near Richmond."[4]

The 52nd was ordered to North Carolina in December 1862, where it was to take part in an expedition against the port city of Wilmington. A violent storm, however, caused the sinking of the most important ship in the flotilla–the U.S.S. *Monitor*—and the attack was called off. Instead, the 52nd was sent to Port Royal, South Carolina, where it would become part of a force that would attempt to reduce the defenses of Charleston. The 52nd would take part in several unsuccessful attacks against the city's defenses for the next year and half. The regiment's soldiers were mere observers, however, during the now-famous attack on Fort Wagner by the Union forces on July 18, 1863, which included the assault of the celebrated 54th Massachusetts (Colored) Infantry.[5]

In December 1863 many of the regiment's soldiers reenlisted and were given a "veteran furlough." Additionally, new enlistments brought the strength of the regiment to 1,000 men. Among these fresh recruits was Private Ezra Ripple, who was mustered into his new unit at Folly Island, South Carolina, on April 15, 1864.[6] Ripple, however, would spend only two and a half months in the 52nd. In a bungled amphibious assault on Fort Johnson, another of the Charleston defenses, the entire contingent of the 52nd's storming party—those who were not killed—was captured after they succeeded in breaching the Confederate defenses. Among the 135 men taken prisoner were the regimental commander, Colonel Henry M. Hoyt, and Private Ezra Ripple.[7] Hoyt would survive incarceration to be breveted to the rank of brigadier general and after the war was elected governor of Pennsylvania. Ripple, too, would survive, and also would gain prominence as the mayor of Scranton, Pennsylvania. But first he would have to endure the horrors of Andersonville and Florence.

Although Andersonville Prison, or "Camp Sumter" as the Confederates called it, did not have the highest mortality rate of all the Civil War prisons, this largest of the Confederate military prisons came to symbolize all that was terrible in this horrendous fratricidal war. Built in 1864 to house the Union enlisted men who had been incarcerated in and around Richmond, Andersonville was designed and constructed to hold a maximum of 10,000 prisoners. When Union prisoners were first brought there in February 1864, the prison compound had been built in the shape of a rectangle comprising about sixteen and a half acres surrounded by a fifteen-foot stockade of pine logs. By the time Private Ripple and his comrades arrived, Camp Sumter—enlarged to twenty six and a half acres in June 1864—was confining over 31,000 Union prisoners.[8]

Ripple found the interior of the stockade to be an unorganized, filthy, smelly sea of starving and decrepit humanity. About twenty paces from the stockade walls was the so-called "deadline," comprised of a series of posts driven into the ground on top of which thin boards were nailed, creating a second, less-imposing barrier but which meant instant death from a guard's bullet to those unfortunate enough to cross or even touch it. Running through the center of the prison was the main source of water, Sweetwater, or Stockade Creek. This small tributary provided the prisoners water with which they could cook their rations and quench their thirst, but it also served as the prison's sewer, carrying off the excrement from the slit latrines that straddled its banks.

Scanty provisions, bad water, lack of shelter, even a dearth of cooking utensils made the plight of the Union prisoners unbearable. Dwindling resources in the Confederacy and poor administration by the Confederate War Department was the cause of most of suffering at Andersonville and other Confederate prisons, not intentional acts of cruelty imposed by the civil and military authorities of the Confederacy, as some ex-prisoners would claim after the war. Perhaps this is what makes Ripple's memoirs somewhat unusual. In an era when the Republican Party never failed to "wave the bloody shirt" in defiance to the Democratic Party—the party of the South—Ripple, a staunch Republican in his own right, held no grudges against the South, its people, and for the most part, his jailers. Of Major Henry Wirz, the commandant of Camp Sumter who was singled out for retribution by the U.S. government after the conflict, Ripple wrote: "One of our boys described Wirz as being the most even-tempered man he ever saw, in that he was always in a rage." After standing trial as a war criminal, Wirz was hanged on November 10, 1865. But in Ripple's mind Wirz was not the main culprit. Instead, he blamed most of the problems at Andersonville on Brigadier General John H. Winder, to whom Wirz reported, and who Ripple believed was the devil incarnate. On the other hand, Ripple remembered some of his guards as being very kindly, and he even hoped to reestablish contact with some of them.

Fortunately, Ripple would spend only two months at Camp Sumter, but approximately 12,000 of his fellow prisoners would never leave, and today occupy Andersonville National Cemetery. For Ripple and his surviving comrades, military incursions by Union forces near Andersonville forced their removal to prison sites less threatened, such as Florence, South Carolina, which—after a layover in Charleston while en route—would become "home" to Ripple for the next seven months. Florence was similar in layout to Andersonville. Encompassing little more than twenty-three acres and enclosed by a stockade of vertical timbers, it, too, had a deadline running around the interior of the palisade. And like the prison at Andersonville, Florence Prison had a stream meandering through the middle of the pen, which the prisoners used for drinking, bathing, and to carry off human waste.[9]

Ripple discovered at Florence that his ability to play the fiddle could make his incarceration a bit easier. Acquiring a violin which another prisoner had brought into the compound, Ripple found that he could get extra rations and other favors by serenading the prison's officers. Believing that his musical performances might be perceived that he was aiding and giving comfort to the enemy, Ripple rationalized that "as I was expected to get some aid and comfort *from* the enemy in return, I thought one would balance the other." At the urging of his comrades, who convinced him there was nothing wrong with taking advantage of a situation that possibly could save his life, Ripple soon formed an "orchestra" of other prisoners with musical abilities. (In another war eighty years later, victims of the Nazi concentration camps also would form musical ensembles for the listening pleasure of their tormentors.)

Because Ripple and his musically talented associates were allowed outside of the prison to play at social functions on nearby plantations, the chances of escape became much more realistic—and tempting. Concerned that they were going to be moved to yet another prison and could thus lose some of the privileges they had earned, Ripple and some of his comrades set out for freedom one night in February 1865, after playing at a dance outside the prison compound. Tracked down by dogs and nearly mauled to death, Ripple survived the ordeal but was punished by the prison authorities for attempting to escape.

With Sherman's troops quickly advancing through South Carolina, it was decided that the prisoners would again be moved, this time to southwest Georgia. When the advancing Union army cut the last rail line to that area, the Confederates' only option was to parole the Yankee prisoners. Transported with the sick and wounded prisoners to Wilmington, North Carolina, Ripple was paroled on March 1, 1865, two days shy of his ninth month in captivity. Ripple could consider himself blessed. While Florence Prison was in operation between September 1864 and March 1865, upward of 18,000 Union prisoners were incarcerated there. Of these 2,802 still lie in the cemetery.[10]

After his release, Ripple traveled to Camp Parole, in Annapolis, Maryland, where former prisoners were bathed, given new uniforms, and received medical attention. He then returned to Scranton on a thirty-day furlough (which was subsequently extended) to allow him time to recuperate. Private Ripple mustered out of the service on June 30, 1865, with a bonus of three months extra pay for his tribulations while a prisoner of war.[11]

After the war, Ripple decided to get a better education and thus entered Eastman's Business College in Poughkeepsie, New York. In 1869 he began working for a firm of crockery dealers and remained with that establishment until 1873, when he became a partner in a coal operations business. He also became a director of the Scranton Axle Works and the *Scranton Tribune.* In addition, Ripple was the secretary/treasurer of the Northern Electric Railroad and also served as a bank director. Ezra married Sarah H. Hackett on April 22, 1874. Together they had five children, one of whom died as an adolescent.[12]

Disturbances in the coal fields led to his enlistment in the Pennsylvania National Guard, and he was elected captain of Company D of the Scranton City Guard when it was organized in 1877. A year later he was elected major of the 13th Regiment of Infantry, Pennsylvania National Guard, becoming lieutenant colonel in 1883 and colonel and regimental commander in 1888. In 1896 he was named Commissary General (while retaining the rank of colonel), and later was appointed the state's assistant adjutant general.[13] His son, Ezra, Jr., later served under his father in the 13th. (Ezra, Jr., was mobilized for active service during the Spanish-American War and World War I.)[14]

Ezra Ripple became active in politics after the Civil War. He was elected county treasurer in 1879 and won Scranton's mayoral election as a Republican in 1886, serving a single term of four years. During his incumbency Scranton began asphalting its streets, modernized them with electric lighting, and established an electric trolley line. Ripple was elected or appointed to many other offices, including his appointment by President McKinley as postmaster of Scranton. He was subsequently reappointed to this position by President Teddy Roosevelt and was still serving in this capacity upon his death from "apoplexy" on November 19, 1909, when he was sixty-six years old.[15] Attending the funeral at Dunmore Cemetery in Scranton were the governor of Pennsylvania and several other dignitaries. "To me he was a dear and intimate friend," said the Commonwealth's governor, "the soul of integrity and type of citizen whose loss will be deeply regretted." The local newspaper called him "Scranton's Best Beloved Citizen."[16]

Another bronze tablet affixed to Pennsylvania's memorial at Andersonville National Cemetery depicts the prisoners reaching over the so-called "deadline" to fill their drinking cups with water from "Providence Spring," which miraculously appeared in answer to the prisoners' prayers for a fresh source of water within the prison compound. The artist who rendered the scene was James E. Taylor, a Civil War veteran of the 10th New York Infantry (National Zouaves). Born in Cincinnati, Ohio, on December 12, 1839, Taylor received his formal art training in New York City just before the outbreak of the Civil War. After two years of service in the 10th New York, where he earned the rank of sergeant, Taylor left the army and became a war correspondent and illustrator for *Leslie's Illustrated Newspaper* during the remaining years of the conflict. His most famous work is the collection of drawings that portray the Shenandoah Valley Campaign of 1864 between General Jubal Early and General Phil Sheridan, which he called *With Sheridan Up the Shenandoah Valley in 1864: Leaves from a Special Artist's Sketch Book and Diary.*[17] After his tenure with Sheridan's army, Taylor followed General Benjamin Butler's Army of the James and finished his wartime endeavors trailing Sherman's forces. Taylor remained with *Leslie's Illustrated Newspaper* until 1883. In the twilight of his career he spent his remaining years working on commission from his studio in New York City and completing *With Sheridan Up the Shenandoah Valley.* James Taylor died in New York City on June 22, 1901, at the age of 62.[18]

It was no coincidence that Taylor's artistic rendering of the Providence Spring scene was chosen to be on the Pennsylvania Memorial. A few years earlier, Ezra Ripple had commissioned Taylor to illustrate his prison memoirs, including the Providence Spring portrayal later cast in bronze on the Pennsylvania Memorial. Originally penned in India ink by Taylor, the illustrations were then photographically reproduced on glass and then hand colored by the artist. These plates were illuminated by a lantern to cast a primitive slide show which Ripple used to accompany presentations—based on these memoirs—initially as a lecture series sponsored by the Scranton YMCA, and later to Grand Army of the Republic meetings and at other patriotic and civic gatherings. The accompanying captions are the original ones, written in the author's own hand. The complete list of captions appears in the back of the book.

Although this book marks the first time that Ripple's complete memoirs have been published, Taylor's illustrations first appeared in a national publication in the October 1964 issue of *American Heritage.* With narrative provided by the great Civil War historian Bruce Catton, the focus of the article clearly was the color illustrations of Taylor, not the words of Ripple, although Catton drew on the memoirs to provide some of the narrative for the text. Catton astutely noted that "Ripple seems to have worked carefully with Taylor, going over the rough drafts of the sketches to make sure that they showed things accurately."[19] Taylor's prison illustrations next appeared in the November 1974 issue of *Civil War Times Illustrated* when, in an article about Florence Prison, excerpts from Ripple's memoirs once again served only to highlight the artist's drawings.[20]

Although Taylor's illustrations make Ripple's memoirs atypical, there were many other ex-prisoners who left written accounts of the horrors they had experienced. Many of their reminiscences were tinged with a burning hatred of their captors, while others wrote as objectively as possible, considering the circumstances. Perhaps the intervention of several decades softened any harsh feelings Ripple might have had toward his former enemy and jailers, or maybe it was the spirit of nationalism that swept the country during the last decade of the nineteenth century and the first decade of the twentieth that allowed Ripple to remember his experiences without bearing a grudge against his fellow Americans. "I wanted to put on record for history's sake that which I knew to be true," concluded Ripple, "and this I have done without malice or exaggeration as God is my judge." Whatever their reasons might have been, Ezra Ripple's prose and James Taylor's artistry have given us a mental *and* visual portrait of the suffering and horror that were Andersonville and Florence.

Mark A. Snell
October 1995

Preface

This book is an edited version of Ezra Hoyt Ripple's Civil War memoirs of his experiences in the Andersonville and Florence prisons. Serena Hinkel, a daughter-in-law of Susan Hinkel, granddaughter of Ezra Hoyt Ripple, previously had retyped and duplicated the original manuscript. Since she made that copy, a bound volume has surfaced which was undoubtedly his final, amended version. The two versions are essentially the same, but there are occasional differences—a few sentences here and there, and several additional paragraphs. Any substantial additions found in the bound copy are included in this published version.

In an effort to maintain the spirit of Ezra Ripple's original memoirs, care was taken to make as few editorial changes as possible. Since these memoirs originally were written as two separate presentations—one about Andersonville and one about Florence Prison—some deletions were made in the beginning of Part Two to avoid redundancy. Additionally, new paragraphing, chapter breaks, some additional punctuation, and upper/lower case corrections were required to give the memoirs greater clarity.

Every attempt was made to identify the numerous individuals mentioned by Ripple in his memoirs. To accomplish this, research was conducted in the Compiled Military Service Records of Civil War soldiers kept at the National Archives. In the case of Union soldiers, their Federal Pension Files at the National Archives also were checked. Additionally, published rosters such as Bates's *History of the Pennsylvania Volunteers* and Henderson's *Roster of the Confederate Soldiers of Georgia* were consulted. Any soldiers positively identified are described in endnotes. In some cases, however, Ripple did not include enough information to allow the editor of these memoirs to properly identify the soldier, such as when only a last name and the soldier's state was given.

I wish to thank Dale Wilson—formerly an editor at Presidio Press now serving as a professor at Valley Forge Military Academy—for recommending me for this project. His replacement at Presidio, E. J. McCarthy, has been a pleasure with whom to work. In addition, Cheryl and David Adam of Seal Literary Agency gave me useful editing advice. I also extend my thanks to Al Pejack of Shepherd College for his help in scanning the original typescript and formatting it for word-processing software. William Lucht, my "boss" at Shepherd, along with my secretary, Irene Moss, both lent an understanding ear during the final editing of the manuscript. D. Scott Hartwig, a historian at Gettysburg National Military Park, and Ted Alexander, a historian at Antietam National Battlefield, provided useful insight, guidance, and information. Amanda Rhodes, Cemetery Director at Andersonville National Cemetery, graciously provided photographs of the Pennsylvania Memorial located there. Thanks also go to Shirley Ropiza of Gettysburg for her assistance in conducting research at the National Archives. And the Archives' Michael Musick, as usual, went "above and beyond the call of duty." Finally, I wish to extend my heartfelt gratitude to Susan Hinkel, granddaughter of Ezra Ripple, for her advice, keen insight, patience, and hospitality.

Notes

Foreword

1. *Pennsylvania at Andersonville Georgia: Ceremonies at the Dedication of the Memorial Erected by the Commonwealth of Pennsylvania in the National Cemetery at Andersonville Georgia* (1909), p.14.

2. Ibid. pp.7, 15.

3. Compiled Military Service Records of Ezra H. Ripple, National Archives, Washington, D.C. (hereafter cited as "Service Record"). Ripple's service record also indicates that he had a florid complexion and had grown to a height of 5 feet, 7½ inches tall. The emergency units to which Ripple belonged were Co. I, 13th Penna. Emergency Militia (Infantry), which was raised in response to the Confederate invasion of Maryland in September 1862; and Co. H, 30th Penna. Emergency Militia (Infantry), called forth by Governor Andrew Curtin to repel the Confederate invasion of Pennsylvania in June 1863. (The information about the emergency units was gleaned from Ripple's Federal Pension File, also located in the National Archives.)

4. Samuel P. Bates, *History of the Pennsylvania Volunteers, 1861–5,* Vol. 3 (Reprinted Wilmington, N.C., 1993), p.51.

5. Ibid. pp.55–56.

6. "Volunteer Enlistment" form of Ezra Ripple. Service Record.

7. *Bates, Pennsylvania Volunteers,* pp.58–60. The 52nd remained in the Charleston area until Sherman's army marched through the Carolinas, upon which the 52nd became part of that army. The 52nd Pennsylvania was mustered out of the federal service at Harrisburg on July 12, 1865.

8. U.S. National Park Service, *Andersonville National Historic Site* (visitors' brochure).

9. G. Wayne King, "Death Camp at Florence," *Civil War Times Illustrated* [hereafter cited as CWTI] (January 1974), p.37.

10. Ibid. p.42.

11. Service Record.

12. "Col. Ezra H. Ripple Claimed by Death," *Scranton Times,* November 19, 1909, pp.1, 14.

13. Ibid.

14. Jack Jackson, "The Splendid Little War with Spain," *The Metro*, May 13, 1994, p.12; and "Pennsylvanians 'Over There': France, 1918," *The Metro*, May 20, 1994, p.13.

15. *Scranton Times*, November 19, 1908, p.14.

16. "Governor Mourner at Col. Ripple's Funeral," *Scranton Times*, November 22, 1909, p.1.

17. *With Sheridan Up the Shenandoah Valley in 1864: Leaves from a Special Artist's Sketch Book and Diary* was not published until 1989 under the title of *The James E. Taylor Sketchbook* (Cleveland: The Western Reserve Historical Society).

18. George F. Skotch, ed., "With a Special in the Shenandoah: From James Taylor's Diary and Sketch Book," *CWTI* (April 1982), p.36.

19. Catton, ed., "A Civil, and Sometimes Uncivil, War," *American Heritage* (October 1964), p.51.

20. King, "Death Camp at Florence," *CWTI* (November 1974), p.35–42.

Introduction

This story of my prison life was undertaken for my wife and children with no expectation of using it beyond the walls of our own home. My purpose now is to commit it to them not to be published until after I am gone. At the solicitation of the Y.M.C.A. of Scranton, it was first made public in a lecture course for that institution. I have aimed to make it truthful both as to text and illustrations, and I think the fact that it is truthful can be established by reference to any who were participants of the scenes it represents. . . . [T]hose who desire the proofs may find plenty in the government publication "Rebellion Records" [*Official Records of the War of the Rebellion*] Volumes 7 and 8, second series.

The first part of my story describes life in Andersonville Prison commencing with our capture and covering a period from July 3rd, to September 13th, 1864; the second part covers from that time to March 1st, 1865, during which time we were in Florence Prison, for a short time outside the stockade and the balance of the time inside. It also gives an account of life outside of the stockade for a short time as a paroled man.

In writing this account I had no data to refer to, nothing beyond a retentive memory on which the incidents had been indelibly impressed. I have read many other accounts of prison life and may have unconsciously adopted the language or style of others, but I have endeavored to make this my own work. Much of it has been written between the hours of 10 and 12 P.M. after a busy day's work. The pictures are photographic copies of the original pictures in India ink by Mr. James E. Taylor of New York City, a celebrated War

Artist and an illustrator of War books and papers. They were made after my description and corrected carefully to make them as true to the facts as possible. If all those who went through prison life in the South, during the Civil War, could relate their experiences, this would be found to be very tame in comparison with many others.

We all suffered, some being of different organization suffered more than others. The suffering and death did not end there. Many came home to suffer for years and then die. Thousands came home only to die within a few days or weeks. Wherever they died, whether at home or in the prison, their lives were given for you who read these pages, and if you appreciate the sacrifice, teach your boys and girls their duty in preserving to posterity this Union for which their lives were so freely given.

                                                    Ezra H. Ripple
                                                    Scranton, Pa.
                                                    August 1902

PART I
Andersonville

Chapter One

This book] is an account of my life and experiences in the prisons of the Southern Confederacy during the Civil War, 1861–65. The war has been over for many years and I have no desire to add to its bitter memories, for we are now a united people and there are many things that occurred on both sides during that terrible war which it were well to allow to pass into oblivion. It is right and proper, however, and necessary to the preservation of the true history of those times, to put on record the patriotism and heroism of the brave defenders of the Union who fought a more desperate fight and against greater odds and with greater losses within the prison pens than did their brave brothers in the open field.

This account, then, is not written with any bitterness of feeling, but, on the contrary, with a desire to eliminate anything of that kind, and to give a true and faithful account of what came under my own observation and my own experience, for the benefit of those who follow me. It is only a simple recital of the recollections of scenes and events in which it was my fortune to take a part, and of which, considering the important bearing they had on the closing scenes of the great rebellion, but little comparatively has been written or said. You are all familiar with the name "ANDERSONVILLE," you have heard that it was a place in which many thousand Union prisoners of war suffered and died, but of the particulars of that suffering and great mortality you can have but little knowledge or conception, unless it had been your fortune to be there. Where hundreds have written of the battles on land and sea for the Union, not more than a score or two have written of the horrors of the Southern prisons. The subject is not a pleasant or attractive one. We would all sooner listen to a description of a grand battle where all the bravery and dash of trained soldiers in assault and defense is portrayed in the most vivid and glowing colors than to a tale which has little in it but that which is revolting, sickening and sorrowful. Yet from Gettysburg to Appomattox Court House there were less Union soldiers killed on the field of battle than died in the prison pens of the South in the same space of time. From about the first of February, 1864, when Andersonville received its first invoice of prisoners, until the end of the war, the total loss, killed in battle of the Union Armies was less than 30,000. During that same time there died in Andersonville, according to the prison records making a total of 30,542 in these four prisons alone.

Andersonville, because of the greater number confined there, overshadows the other prisons, but the mortality there was not as great in proportion as in some other prisons. Salisbury with its 12,000 nearly all in unknown graves; Florence with over 2,800; Millen with nearly as many; Richmond, Danville, Belle Isle, Columbia, Blackshear, and other prisons on this side of the Mississippi, Camp Ford, Texas, and others on the other side, all contributed their quota to the grand total which placed the name of the Union soldier far above all others for deeds of heroic sacrifice and steadfast loyalty to country. The terrible mortality in Southern prisons was not distributed over the whole war as the losses in the field were, but was in a great measure included in the last year of the war.

The cartel of exchange between the Union and Confederate Armies was broken sometime during the year 1863, and from that time until the operations of General Sherman in the early part of 1865 compelled the rebels to run their prisoners through to our lines and parole them there, to avoid their being released by him—with the exception of a special exchange of 10,000 in November and December 1, 1864—there was no exchange of prisoners. There was no time during the war when there were so many prisoners taken on both sides as during this time, and as they began to accumulate at Richmond and other centers in the Confederacy, the rebel authorities found themselves obliged to provide for their accommodation elsewhere. It was decided to concentrate them in Georgia, and Andersonville, being at the time secure from any incursions of our troops, was the place selected.

The prison was about twenty-five acres in area, 750 or 800 feet one way, by 1,500 the other way. The prison was in a valley, the sides gently sloping to the center through which ran a stream of water ten or fifteen feet in width. On the northerly side of the stream there was quite a bog taking up from three to five acres of the prison. The hills surrounding the prison were quite heavily wooded with yellow pine timber. Andersonville was only a way station, there being no town there, the nearest place of any importance being Americus, about ten miles distant.

After the lapse of over thirty years, the recollections of many of the scenes and events which I may attempt to describe are necessarily somewhat dimmed, and the names of many of those who passed through the furnace of affliction with me have been forgotten, but the greater part of the scenes and incidents coming under my observation they are so indelibly impressed on my memory that while reason, sense, or life remains they can never be effaced.

My regiment, the 52nd Penna., was one of an expedition organized under General Foster, to get possession of James Island in Charleston Harbor, and either hold it or spike the guns of Fort Johnson, and allow our fleet to get through and compel the surrender of Charleston. The attack failed and all of us who landed, about 140 in number, were either killed or captured. Our Colonel (Ex-Gov. Hoyt), Lt. Col. John B. Conyngham, and Adjutant [1st Lieutenant Silas A.] Bunyan were among the prisoners, the two former slightly and the latter mortally wounded. It was the morning of the 3rd of July, 1864, just at daybreak, that we walked into the Confederacy over the parapets of Fort Johnson, and it was not until the first of the following March that I was privileged to shake the acquaintance thus hastily and rashly formed.[1]

Of my company there were four besides myself captured and as I will have to refer to them hereafter by name, I will take occasion to introduce them to you now. John Rapp of Reading, Pa., a brave boy of only about twenty years of age, but a veteran of tried courage, and an unselfish and true friend under all circumstances. I have never met him since the war, and have only within a short time learned of his whereabouts. He is now in Nevada City, Cal., where he went as soon as he was discharged from the army. He has served five terms

Attack on Fort Johnson July 3ᵈ 1864

as Recorder of Nevada County, which attests the regard and confidence in which they hold him there.[2] Michael Beavers of Hyde Park [a suburb of Scranton], now dead, a man well advanced in years at the time, but hardy and strong until broken down by suffering. He was a true patriot and when offered warm clothing and plenty to eat if he would take service with the Confederates, spurned the offer with indignation, although the chances were ten to one that he would die within the month.[3] John Brennan of Schuylkill Co., lately in the Soldiers' Home at Erie, Pennsylvania, but now dead, a little redheaded Irishman who could eat mush boiling hot without winking or shedding a tear, and who seemed to hold us in a state of contemptuous regard because our mouths were too tender to follow his lead. Despite this failing, he was a good fellow and a brave soldier.[4] Bill Goodman, not worthy of notice, a substitute, a thief, and a fraud. He died in prison and we who were the victims of his thievish propensities wished many a time that he had died before he got there.[5]

I had very few other acquaintances among the boys outside of my own company, as I had only been with the regiment a short time, and as only four others of Company K were captured, I was almost like a stranger among those who had been captured with me. Owing to my nearsightedness, I had not been put on regular duty in the Company, but acted as Company Clerk and did such other duty as was assigned me. When it became known that the expedition was to take place, I was anxious to go with my regiment and through Lieut. Henry A. Mott, my Company Commander, obtained permission of Colonel Hoyt to accompany the regiment as Bugler.

The attack was to be made in small boats, and by the orders of the Colonel I accompanied him and was to stay by him, and if it became necessary to retreat I was to blow the bugle, and only in case of retreat was it to be blown. Had there been occasion to blow it, I would have failed utterly, because whether carried away by shot or otherwise lost, when I turned the bugle over to the rebs there was no mouthpiece in it. Delayed in finding the channel when we arrived in front of Fort Johnson, Colonel Hoyt ordered our boat ahead, and taking the advance we piloted such boats as eventually made a landing, over the [sand] bar. Being in the bow of the boat, it was my fortune to be the first to land, which I did, Rapp immediately following waist-deep in the water, and we together hauled the boat up so that the Colonel and others landed dry-shod. As the Colonel left the boat he picked up Mike Beavers' gun and calling on the others to follow charged up the beach towards the Fort. Previous to this time they in the Fort had discovered our attack and the fire from the Fort was now getting hot. The Colonel, forgetting the guns were not capped, snapped the lock, and as it failed to go off, threw it from him in disgust. I picked it up and immediately forgot my orders to stay by him. He went towards the lower part of the Fort and I turned in the other direction in search of someone of whom to borrow a . . . [percussion] cap. I got one from one of the boys and got a chance to empty my gun over the parapet of the Fort. Just then I recollected my orders and started to find the Colonel.

When we were surrendered, which was not done until after there was absolutely no hope of victory or escape for us, and our men were being rapidly shot down without chance to retaliate, we were formed in column and marched into one of the bombproofs, where we were kept until the fire from our forts had slackened, when we were marched out, counted, and sent under a heavy guard over to Charleston. I had a brand new canteen, nicely covered, which struck the fancy of one of our guards and he bantered me to trade with him for his. He had an old tin one with no cover, and, as I afterwards found, filled with half decayed orange peelings. I have never been much of a trader at any time, and I was not particularly anxious to trade canteens, but this particular guard had such a *taking* way with him that I was finally induced to trade. That same old canteen, poor as it was, did me excellent service during the following eight months. A canteen in prison was a valuable article, not so much for holding or carrying water as for other purposes. A canteen divided at the soldering line would make two excellent frying pans. These pans would also answer to bake corn meal dodgers in, would do duty as plates, and were excellent scoops for digging tunnels.

In the attack on the Fort we had lost about one-fourth our number killed and wounded. Of our boat load, ten in number, two were killed and one wounded. We were taken over to Charleston during the morning, where we received quite an ovation. On arriving there we were marched through the part of the city which was exposed to the fire of our guns on Morris Island, to the city prison. On our way there through the burned district, we passed the building in which the Union officers were kept under the fire of our own guns, and as we passed they came out on the portico to see us march by. We gave one cheer but were prevented from any further demonstration by our guards. General Dana of the 143rd Penna. Vols. was among the number and was recognized by some of our boys.[6]

On the way to the prison we were subjected to all sorts of taunts and chaffing, and many of the titles given us were not such as are usually found in Sunday school books. We took it all in as good part as we could and said as little as possible. But sometimes we could not refrain from returning in kind the slurs cast upon us. In Charleston and in other cities through which we passed, the hatred felt for us was very plainly shown, and there was a great disposition to forget what was due us as prisoners of war. It is due to our guards, however, to state that nothing further than bad language towards us was permitted. We were taken into the jail yard, where we put in a most miserable day. The consciousness of being prisoners weighed heavily on

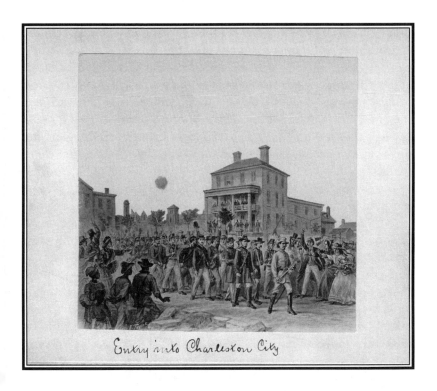

Entry into Charleston City

us; the weather was hot, and in that jail yard not a breath of cool air could get to us. Very often during the day we could hear the swish of the shells coming over from our batteries on Morris Island, and several exploded not very far from our prison. The firing kept up with very little intermission all day and during the night. In the middle of the afternoon a tub full of boiled mush with some bacon was brought in, but very few partook of it to any great extent; our stomachs were too proud as yet. I often thought afterwards of that scorned tub of mush and wished for the opportunity to attack it. Towards evening we were taken into the jail and being tired and feeling very sad, I lay down on the stone floor of the cell and soon went to sleep.

We came into Charleston from the sand hills of Morris Island full of fleas, but the first night in prison was the last we saw of them. The lice attacked them in overwhelming numbers, drove them off, and took possession of our bodies. From a very intimate and prolonged acquaintance with these plagues I much prefer the active, sprightly, vivacious though wicked flea. The other fellow is not so active or graceful in his movements but he is more persistent in his attacks and he gets there just the same, and if anything more so. To one who loves the chase, the pursuit of the flea offers considerable sport. For his size he puts up as game a fight as a bobcat or mountainlion, and until you get accustomed to hunting him and know something of his tricks, he will keep you guessing.

I arose early the next morning and investigated the cell and found in it an old "Prison Record" which I examined with much interest. On one page I found an entry where a man had been imprisoned for thirty days for killing a negro, and on the opposite page another had been sent up for six months for vagrancy and expressing abolition sentiments. As I had no paper and knew I would need some, I tore out this leaf, folded it up a number of times, and made a diary of it. On it I recorded the deaths of many of my comrades who died in prison, and much data which would now be of great value if I had it, but unfortunately it was stolen from me in Florence prison during the following winter. I had some of the best cake recipes in that old diary that ever were heard of. When we were very hungry we used to exchange cake recipes, etc., with each other, and we would take them down as carefully as if we had all the ingredients at hand to make them, and we would resolve within ourselves if we ever lived to get home, about the first thing we would do would be to have a big lot of those things cooked, baked, boiled or fried under our own supervision and give them a good soul-satisfying test ourselves.

We remained in Charleston prison and jail yard until the morning of the 6th, when we were taken out and put on board the cars for Andersonville. At the present time, the journey from Charleston to Andersonville can be made in a few hours, but it was a very long and tiresome journey then to us, for we did not arrive at Andersonville until the morning of the 8th. The railroads throughout the Confederacy at this time were in a very poor condition, there being no material with which to repair them and labor to keep them up was also scarce, so that riding over them was both uncomfortable and dangerous.

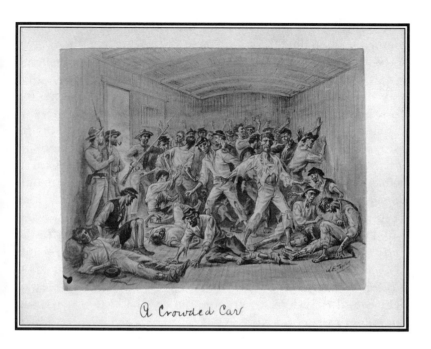

A Crowded Car

We were put in box cars, about forty and fifty in a car and one door was closed and the guards, three or four to a car, stood in the doorway of the other side. In this crowded condition with no ventilation, in the heat of summer, we were carried on our way, full of the misery of the present but having little conception of what was before us. We were guarded the most of our way by a company of cadets from the South Carolina Military Institute in Charleston City—the Citadel Cadets. They were fine-looking fellows, from 18 to 20 years of age, well officered and well drilled, and as far as my observation went they treated us with a great deal of consideration. They were very gentlemanly and kind to us and when they engaged in conversation with any of us were very careful not to be offensive in their remarks or to needlessly hurt our feelings. We had experience afterwards with other kinds of guards and came to know from sad experience the difference between gentlemen and true soldiers, and the cruel, inhuman rabble which could not be trusted at the front, where there was danger, but were given the comparatively safe duty of guarding helpless and starving prisoners. I had no acquaintance while in

Andersonville with the soldiers of the 5th or 55th Georgia who guarded us for a time there, but came to know some of them while at Florence, S.C., and found a good many good fellows among them, and that, with few exceptions, they were as considerate of us as they were allowed to be. They were soldiers who had seen service at the front and had gained some respect for an enemy.[7]

Whenever we stopped at any town the people would flock to the train to see the "Yanks" and they would talk about us in our presence as if we were devoid of sense or hearing. They seemed to regard us as they would cattle. There were very few men among them, mainly women and children, black and white. Of the white some would look on us with scorn, some would scold and berate us, while a very few would drop us now and then a word of comfort or pity. But in the eyes of one class there was always that look which said to us as plainly as *words* could say it, "we pity you," "we are your friends, for we know it is for our sakes you are suffering." The poor blacks powerless to help us could only look the gratitude and sympathy they would fain put into words and actions.

At Augusta, John Rapp bought a quart of milk and divided it with Brennan, Beavers, and myself. We were thirsty, hot, and half-suffocated, and the milk was good beyond description. The price came near beyond description too. It took two dollars of Rapp's scanty pile. If we had known it, we could have exchanged our "Green-Backs" for "Greybacks" (Confederate money) in about the proportion of three or four for one and could have bought as much with a dollar of Confederate money as with a dollar Greenback. This knowledge came to us further on.

As illustrating the bitter feeling entertained for us by some, one of my comrades relates the following story. He says the incident came under his own observation. An old lady came up to the cars at Augusta and by permission of the guards engaged in conversation with the boys. She asked many questions about our capture, etc., and would often say "What a pity, what a pity" and this at times where it did not seem to be appropriate and where her actions and her words were not in harmony. At last one of the boys asked her why she used these words so often and in the manner in which she did. She answered, I will tell you. "You have come down here to burn our homes, to destroy our country and to kill our young men, and I say instead of your lives being spared and you made prisoners, what a pity it is you had not been killed on the battlefield instead, and your bodies left there to enrich the land you came to destroy."

The story is so much like the expressions we were accustomed to hearing that I have no reason to doubt the truth of it. Now, after years have passed away, and the heat and bitterness of the strife have given way to calm reason and sober thought, I do not wonder at the bitterness in the hearts of those people. What did any principle amount to, to these women whose fathers, sons, and brothers were battling with us. All they knew or cared for was that their loved ones were being killed, maimed, sent to Northern prisons, or sent home to die from wounds or disease incurred in the war we were prosecuting, and it was not in human nature that they *should* love us. Our mothers and sisters wasted but very little love on *rebel* soldiers as a rule.

At some point between Charleston and Macon we were told that about the time of the breaking out of the war the road had been laid with foreign rails on one side, and American rails on the other, in order to test their relative worth and durability. I never learned which came out ahead, it could not have been that which was laid on our side of the track, for it was rough enough to shake our teeth loose.

At Macon we were separated from our officers, they remaining there, I believe, while we were sent on. The officers and enlisted men were never confined together, and the officers were always allowed privileges which were not granted the men.[8] They also received much better treatment than the enlisted men received. Colonel Hoyt escaped in a short time after his capture and got within sight of our gunboats on the Edisto River, but there the dogs treed him and he was recaptured. He was exchanged by a special exchange in less than two months from the date of his capture and returned to his command. In the meantime a stockade had been erected on Morris Island for rebel prisoners and he was placed in charge of it. It might have been expected that he would have retaliated on them for the cruelties practiced on us, but his naturally kind heart would not suffer him to do this and the prisoners under him fared as well probably as in any prison in the North.

We arrived in Andersonville on the morning of the 8th of July. We

Captain Wirz straitening line

were marched down to the Headquarters of the prison and put
through a thorough search. We were allowed to retain all sums of
money less than a hundred dollars. Very little money was found on
us, however, as precaution had been taken to hide it where there was
not much danger of its being discovered. After having been searched
we were again formed in line and counted off in detachments of
ninety men each, which detachments were subdivided into messes
of thirty men each for convenience in distributing rations.

Sergeant Leander Overpeck of Company F was made Sergeant of
our detachment, and Sammy Smith of Company "I" was placed in
charge of our mess.[9] It was at this time I first saw Captain Henry Wirz,
made famous, or infamous, rather, by his administration as commandant of Andersonville prison. He was a thin, wizened specimen
of a man, resembling in appearance a Skye Terrier (the comparison
is rather unfair to the dog, I will admit), utterly heartless, and hold-

ing his position for that reason, by the full knowledge and purpose of his superiors. His brows were contracted in an angry scowl and he stormed up and down the lines as he tried to get us in the position he wanted. One of our boys described Wirz as being the most even tempered man he ever saw, in that he was always in a rage. He wore a large navy revolver on a belt in a very conspicuous manner, and altogether he was about as fierce and unsociable a specimen of Confederate as I ever met. He used very rough language to us and was very irritable and unreasonable. One of our boys objected to some act of his and made a remark to the effect that Uncle Sam would have something to say about our treatment hereafter. Wirz answered "never you mind, you are not under Uncle Sam now, you are under Uncle Sheff" and we were beginning to realize truly that this was the case.

Chapter Two

We had none of us any knowledge of, nor had we ever heard much of Andersonville, as it had only been in existence a very few months, so that we did not yet realize what we were coming to. This knowledge began to dawn on us very soon, however, for on our way to the prison we soon came to a point of ground overlooking the stockade, where the whole inside of the prison was in full sight below. The effect was stunning and very disheartening. Here was an enclosure fenced about with a stockade of pine timbers comprising about 20 or 25 acres altogether, in the center of which was a bog through which the stream ran which furnished the prison with water. At frequent intervals all around the stockade overlooking the prison were sentry boxes in which the guards were placed. Every inch of space therefore in the prison was directly under their eyes.

When we looked down on the prison it resembled an immense anthill teeming with life. There were about 25,000 prisoners in there at that time, and that mass was swarming and moving about over the face of the prison, on which not a particle of vegetation could be seen, the surface trampled as hard as the floor of a brick yard, and resembling a half-burned brick in color.[10] What a sinking of the heart there was when we came to realize that this was to be our home—no one knew how long—perhaps until the end of the war, whenever that might be. It was not until we had passed the gate and got inside the prison that we came fully to know the dreadful lot into which the fortunes of war and the inhumanity of our captors, had cast us. Filth, disease, starvation, and death were all about us and in forms and shapes that we had never heard of or seen before.

Immediately on our entrance we were warned of the deadline by the old prisoners, no intimation of this institution having previously been made by the guard to us. The "deadline" was originally a railing of a single small strip of wood about a rod inside the stockade running all around the prison, being about three feet high. In some places the fence remained, in others it had been broken down, but in all places where it was or should have been the penalty was death for crossing it or leaning on it or standing on it. Scarcely ever was a warning given by the guard; if a prisoner unwittingly crossed the deadline, as soon as a bead could be drawn on him, sometimes at hardly twenty feet distance, the leaden messenger was sent which released him from his captivity. Many poor fellows, desperate and crazed, deliberately went to their deaths in this way.

It is not my purpose, if I could, to make this more horrible than it was. There was much to be seen there every day so horrible that it

Shot at the dead-line

goes beyond my power to describe it. The treatment which sent
nearly 13,000 out of this one prison to their graves in one year must
have produced horrible scenes. In stating this I want you to understand that 33,206 was the greatest number ever confined there in any
one month. It had been growing up to that point from the time the
prison was opened in February until the month of August. After that
time they began moving them to other prisons until towards the last
there was not a tenth of that number there. The deaths in Andersonville were:

In April 1864 1 out of every 16
In May 1864 1 out of every 26
In June 1864 1 out of every 22
In July 1864 1 out of every 18
In August 1864 1 out of every 10.06
In September 1864 1 out of every 3 (In this month they com-
menced moving us to other prisons, leaving mainly the
sick and disabled.)
In October 1864 1 out of every 2.7 (In this month and Novem-
ber the conditions were much the same, no new prisoners
being brought in.)
In November 1864 1 out of every 2.7
In December 1864 1 out of every 29 (In December Shermans
field of operations having passed beyond Andersonville,
they began moving the prisoners back from the other
prisons to this prison so that the proportions of deaths
very much decreased.)
In January 1865 1 out of every 25
In Febuary 1865 1 out of every 39
In March 1865 1 out of every 28
In April 1865 1 out of every 2 (In this month the prison was
practically abandoned, the prisoners taken to our lines
and paroled, and such only left in the prison as were unable to move or could not be moved, and they were
buried there. Of the 51 left there 32 died.)

The official records of the prison show that the total number received in the prison were 49,485. The number of deaths were 12,926,
showing the percentage of deaths to be 26. Of the number removed

to Florence and Millen [Prison, Georgia] fully 5,000 more died, which would make the total of deaths of those who had originally entered Andersonville nearly 18,000 and the percentage of deaths to be 36.

There is no doubt in my mind that the prison records are far short of the truth, for they state that the greatest number of deaths in any one day (August 23, 1864) to have been 97. I counted the dead myself that day as they lay in line from the south gate to the east side of the stockade and they were over a hundred, and this has been confirmed to me by others since who also counted them. The records themselves show that the average daily deaths in August 1864 were 97. . . .[11]

Several years ago during the prevalence of "La Grippe" I read of the great alarm which had seized the people of Chicago by reason of the great mortality attending the progress of this new and dreaded disease. The account stated that the undertakers were overtaxed and many bodies lay for days awaiting burial. One hundred and sixty-nine had died in one day and for three or four days in succession it had not varied much from that figure. The people were alarmed and ready to flee from the city as if it were plague-stricken. When you come to figure up the results by days and months the figures are really startling. One hundred and sixty-nine in one day gives 5,239 in a [31 day] month, 61,685 in a year. What an army to bury, what sorrow and suffering it represents. Now let us compare it with Andersonville, bearing in mind that Chicago contained eleven hundred thousand souls and Andersonville in August 1864 contained 33,000 prisoners. In that month the dead numbered, according to the prison records, 2,992, or within a fraction of an average of 97 per day for every day in the month. At this rate of mortality, what would have been the death rate of Chicago—3,332 as against 169 per day—99,733 as against 5,239 per [31 day] month, 1,180,000 as against 61,685 per annum. I have made the comparison in order that you may realize how much greater the chances were for dying than living in Andersonville. And what I say of Andersonville will apply equally well to almost every military prison in the South during the last year of the war.

I went down to the south gate the day the greatest number of dead were taken out. From the gate back to the other side of the prison, over seven hundred feet, taking up the entire space in continuous though not compact lines the dead men lay, 144 in number. It was a sad sight as they lay there with their poor, gaunt faces turned up to the glare of the midsummer sun. It was death in all its repulsiveness and horror. When a person would die, some of his comrades would prepare his body for burial by tying his two big toes together, straightening out his limbs, and folding his hands, carefully removing from his person anything that would be of service in the prison, clothing, etc., and then on a small scrap of paper would write his name, company, regiment, and cause of death and would attach it to his collar. As the dead wagons came for them, they were tossed on them like logs of wood, twenty or more on a wagon, and were carted to the burial ground. Here the burial squad would receive them and lay them in trenches about three feet deep, seven feet wide, and a hundred and twenty-five long, placing at the head of each one a slab or rive on which would be cut a number corresponding with the number of the death record. They were laid down side by side, and the earth shoveled over them. No coffins, no other covering, nothing that would bear resemblance to a Christian burial. How precious should this grand inheritance of a preserved Union be to us all when we realize the fearful price that has been paid for it.

In order that you may have some understanding of the causes which produced this terrible mortality, I will endeavor to make some explanation of the situation. First, there was no shelter provided, and we were exposed to the rays of the sun in those hot midsummer days, during the day, and to the dews of the night, with the rain and storms which at that time of the year visited us very often. Then the food was not sufficient to sustain life or keep up health or strength. The food itself was not healthful, and was particularly unfitted for men having any complaints of the bowels. There was no attention paid to the sanitary requirements of the prison, no drainage, no efforts to keep it clean, and no provisions made for the care of the sick inside the prison. After the prison became so crowded, we had no opportunity to bathe or even wash our clothing. Perhaps we would not have washed our clothing a great deal if we had had the water, because the wear and tear of laundrying [sic] clothes is sometimes as great as the actual wear on the person and we were not so rich in clothing as to want to run any needless risk in wearing it out too soon. I did try washing my shirt once shortly after I came in the prison while the spirit of cleanliness was strong in me as yet, but I did not repeat it again while I was in prison. When I put that shirt in the wash it was an able-bodied shirt, it could even stand alone, but when it came out it was a poor, miserable, limp wreck that had no body at all.

The drinking water was scarce, and it was foul with the drainage of the camps inside and outside the stockade. The exposure by day and night, the scarcity and quality of food and water, the filth abounding everywhere, the number of the sick, the entire absence of medical relief, and the crowded condition of the prisons gives full and sufficient answer to the question, why was the mortality so great. In those hot, close days, how we did long for a nice, cool bath. We talked over it the same as we did over the rations until it became a nightmare to us. We had frequent thunderstorms, and one day as we saw one beginning to gather in the distance one of the boys suggested that we strip and get a bath in that way. The idea struck us all at once as a good one and we adopted it. Stripping and placing our clothes in the center of what we called our tent, we awaited the approaching shower. It came up at last from the west in great black clouds and soon the rain was dashing over us in fine style. For a few minutes we wondered why we had not thought of this before. It nearly took our breath away, but we thought we enjoyed it. The water seemed, however, to be unusually cold, we never knew rainwater was so cold.

Like the old fellow who was said to have refused Noah's invitation to get into the Ark, we thought the rain would not last long, as it was only a shower, but we forgot one peculiarity about the showers down there, they seem to make a business of boxing all points of the compass before they get through, and this shower followed the usual custom. It commenced about four P.M. and went from west to north, and to the east and to the south and back again to the west, and did not get through until after dark. In the meantime our clothes had gotten wet through by the rain pouring through a crack between the blankets, and we came about as near freezing to death between that time and daylight as I ever want to. We never tried it again.

When I say there were 33,000 prisoners confined there, it must be understood that it meant 33,000 men, a greater number of able-bodied men fit for military service than there are today in the cities of Scranton and Wilkes Barre combined or perhaps in the County of Lackawanna [Pennsylvania].[12] When you count out the women and children, it takes a very large city to furnish 33,000 able-bodied men, and these men were largely captured from the toughest, hardiest men in the army, men who had been inured to hardships and sufferings before they were captured, and were calculated to endure as much as any men on the face of the earth could endure. It does not need much argument to show that the treatment must have been of the most severe and cruel nature to have broken down and killed so many such men in such a short space of time. We were turned loose in the prison, strangers to all there, and obliged to hunt places for ourselves wherever we could find a vacant spot. The result was we were scattered all through the pen and some of my comrades who were captured with me became so far separated from me that I never met them again while we were in prison.

It is a desolate feeling to be alone in such a multitude and such a hungry, selfish multitude as this was. I was very fortunate in meeting an old friend, Perry Fuller of Hyde Park, immediately after getting inside the prison.[13] He had been in prison a month or more and his experience was of great service to us. He took us to the north side of the prison, where it was not so crowded and helped us to get as good a location as was to be had. Brennan and I had each a rubber blanket which we had been permitted to bring in with us, and with these tied together and suspended over some sticks we were able to obtain some slight shelter from the intense heat of the sun and the soaking dews of the night. We took in with us three Company "I" men of our regiment, and a Michigan cavalryman, making nine in all. It is impossible to make two small gum blankets cover nine men, but at night we all laid with our heads together under the blankets and our feet and legs sticking outside like the spokes of a wheel.

Perry Fuller instructed us in the mysteries of making corn meal balls (recipe not for sale), and did us many kindnesses. He hunted up all the Hyde Park and Scranton boys and brought them around to see us, and told us of all the points of interest. Among other things

Nine sleeping under two gum blankets

he told us of the Indian sharpshooters who had been with Burnside, and who were located in the northwest part of the stockade.[14] I had a great curiosity to see them, and following his directions, I went over on that side one day to hunt them up. There was little or no regularity observed in locating our tents or shelters, and in going around through the prison we were obliged to move with great care. I found the Indians at last and satisfied my curiosity, but in stepping around I did not observe the handle of a pan in which there was some bacon and meal cooking over a little fire. I struck the handle with my foot and dumped its contents into the fire. If a man has any instincts of a gentleman he will apologize when he kicks a man's dinner into the fire, but he wants to be able to hold that man at arm's length while he is doing it. Now, these Indians had arms, as they seemed to me, to be about a foot longer than mine, and the whole gang started on the jump towards me and the frying pan. I recognized at once that this was no time for either apology or explanation, and more

than that I did not know a word of Indian language, and was entirely
unacquainted with Indian fighting, so that prudence dictated that I
had better retire in as good order as was consistent with great celer-
ity of movement, and return some other day when the excitement
had subsided and proffer the pipe of peace. Acting on this impulse,
I jumped over a tent and I think made an eighth of a mile in about
an eighth of a minute in the direction of my friends. I do not know
what became of the Indians. My curiosity having been fully satisfied,
I never went back.

On the eleventh day of July, three days after our arrival, a grand
tragedy was enacted in full view of the largest audiences ever assembled on an occasion of the kind in this country. The starvation,
exposure, and disease were not the only evils with which the prisoners had to contend, and the rebel guards were not the only ones
whose hands were lifted against them. There were those of our own
men who were more cruel and bloodthirsty than even the rebels had

Escaping from Burnside's Indians

ever been. Almost with the first lot of prisoners who came to Andersonville were some of a gang of the meanest villains that ever escaped the gallows. They were bounty jumpers, would-be deserters, and thieves and criminals from the slums of the big cities, and they banded together to rob their weaker fellow prisoners of what money or valuables, blankets, clothing, or anything else they might have that would be worth stealing. With the proceeds of their robberies they bought extra rations and kept themselves well fed while their miserable victims were daily losing strength and courage. With nearly every fresh arrival of prisoners there would be other villains of the same kind added to the gang, until they constituted a powerful and vicious organization, which kept in awe and subjection all the rest of the prisoners.

Whenever the gate would be opened to admit a fresh batch of prisoners, a number of these toughs would be there to spot them. Noting their condition, if they showed signs of having money, or were possessed of good clothing or blankets, they would keep track of them and at night would visit them and take what they had. If they resisted they would be unmercifully beaten, or, as was the case in some instances, killed. It was useless to complain, there was no protection against this hellish crew. At last driven to desperation, a few determined men banded together and resolved that they would break up this murderous gang or die in the attempt. A short time previous to our arrival the two forces came into collision, and they had a series of hard and bloody fights. Right finally prevailed and six of the most desperate and prominent members of the "Raiders" as they were called, were captured and turned over to the rebel authorities for safekeeping, while the "Regulators" empaneled a jury and tried them.

Everything was conducted in the most orderly manner. Proofs of their evil work were plenty, and after a fair trial they were found guilty and sentenced to be hung. The gallows was erected near the south gate (the main gate) and when all was ready the prisoners were brought in and turned over to the "Regulators," Captain Wirz washing his hands entirely of the whole matter. There in the presence of 25,000 fellow prisoners they suffered the just penalty of their crimes. One of them broke away from those having him in charge as they approached the gallows, and tried to escape by getting in the crowd, but he was recaptured. Another broke the rope as he fell, but he did not get free. The rope was again tied around his neck and he was hung for certain the next time. The gang was broken up and no more trouble was occasioned by them. This was on the 11th day of July 1864, and was a rather startling introduction to our prison life. From that time on we had peace and good order within the stockade walls of the prison, if we didn't have much of anything else.[15]

At this time the Army of the Potomac in the East was pushing Lee for all he was worth, while Sherman, Thomas, Howard, Logan, and the brilliant fighters in the Southwest were driving all before them. Each day had its battle or battles and each day sent its quota of prisoners into the stockades throughout the South, so that while death was busy at work reducing our numbers in prisons, the fortunes or misfortunes of war were more than supplying our losses, and each day our numbers steadily and largely increased. I cannot describe to you the horrors of our prison life at this time. A walk through the

Hanging of the raiders

prison would disclose suffering, disease, and death in more awful forms than the mind of man unused to such sights could imagine. The majority of the prisoners were strangers to each other. They had been captured in small detachments, and from many different points. Some had been captured singly and had no friends or acquaintances in the prison. While they were in health and could take care of themselves they could get along as well as the rest, but when they began to fail in health and became unable to help themselves, their condition was pitiable in the extreme. If they had no special trusted friend to draw their rations for them and help them as they needed help, they would soon get in a condition where they would be overrun with lice and would finally be killed by them. It was a blessing for the poor soul who could die and be relieved of his misery before he got to this point, but with some, nature fought hard against death and in such the extreme of suffering and misery was reached before the blessed relief would come. Horrible as it may seem to you, I have myself seen poor fellows lying out in the blazing sun, too weak to help themselves in the least, unable to turn themselves, lying face up, the maggots feasting on them and the lice devouring them. They probably had no friends left to look after them, no one who had known their names, or to what detachment they belonged, and when they were carried out to the dead house, they were recorded as "unknown."

In Andersonville the unknown dead numbered over 921, in some other prisons much more, while in Salisbury [North Carolina] out of twelve thousand buried there, nearly all were marked "unknown." Not only did they keep no burial records in the latter prison but in burying the prisoners they laid them in trenches three deep. It was very little we could do for the relief of the poor souls we would find in this condition. To brush off the worms, turn them over so as to shield their faces from the sun and to give them a drink of water was about all that could be done. While one would do this for them, hundreds would pass them without giving more than a passing glance. You may say that it is hard to believe that human beings would pass by such cases without stopping to help, but you must understand that it was not one or two cases of this kind which would be met, but there were hundreds of them and the senses were soon blunted by such sights, and again, starvation rapidly brutalizes men and robs them of sympathy and all kindly feelings which raise the man above the brute. Starvation will sap the courage as well as the strength of a man and will bring to the surface all the mean and selfish qualities in his nature.

During this time the rebels, being probably unable to furnish cooked rations to the great number confined, found it necessary to issue a certain proportion of rations uncooked, but did not in all cases issue wood to cook them. The consequence was that every scheme was practiced that could be thought of to get wood. The best and most popular way was to help carry a dead man out to the dead house. This being outside of the stockade, permission was given the prisoners on returning to carry some wood with them. If a comrade was very sick and likely to die, much interest would be manifested in his condition by those in his immediate neighborhood, and long before his death, his friends would be besieged by requests to allow others to carry him out when the time would come.

We were not unlike our fellows. About four feet from where we lay there were four Massachusetts Artillerymen, one an elderly man by the name of Emory.[16] I did not like these men, they were ugly to each other and quarreled nearly all the time. Finally poor Emory began to fail and he rapidly grew helpless, and it was evident that he soon would pass over the border. We all watched him and although we really pitied him and did what little favors we could to make him comfortable, we nevertheless made our calculations on forming part of the detail that would carry him out of the stockade. Our necessities required wood, we had no money to buy it, it was not issued to us in sufficient quantity, and as we knew that Emory could not possibly get well, that death was preferable to the condition he was passing through, we hoped the time would not be long. It is an awful thing to calculate and speculate on a person's demise in order to come into an inheritance, but unfortunately this is the way of the world, and it has not been confined to Andersonville. Sammy Smith, one of the Company "I" boys, obtained the consent of Emory's comrades to help carry him out when the time would come. It came one morning early, and Sammy joined the bearers and assisted in carrying poor old Emory out. We had made great calculations on that

Sammy Smith strikes a Sink hole

wood and we anxiously watched for the return of Sammy. After a long time we saw him coming. He was a small man, but he gathered such a big load of brush, and piled it on a board which he was carrying on his head, to such a height, that we could see the wood moving along over the tops of the tents a hundred yards distant while he was entirely hidden from sight. At last he came where we could see his face and it fairly shone with the consciousness of a good work nearly completed. Alas, for all human calculations. There were innumerable sinkholes all through the prison. They were two or three feet in depth and from six to eight inches in diameter. Their presence made it necessary at all times to exercise great care in moving around through the camp. When Sammy was about sixty feet from us, and before we could get to him, he disappeared suddenly from view, a foul smell rose upon the already overburdened air, the wood flew in all directions, and in less than a minute there wasn't as much wood in sight as would have made a toothpick. Sammy had struck a hole.

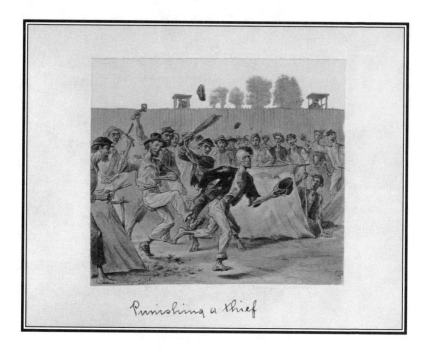

Punishing a Thief

We retired to our tent disconsolate, and Sammy retraced his steps to the creek. Poor Sammy is dead now, but he will never be forgotten. As far as the returns have been received, three widows mourn his loss. He loved not wisely but too many.

There was a general understanding in prison, an unwritten law, that while a man had possession of any property he would not be disturbed in his enjoyment of it, but if he parted company with his property but for an instant, there was danger that he might never see it again. So it was with the wood. While it was on Sammy's head, not a hand was raised to take a splinter of it, but when it struck the ground Sammy lost all ownership, and his property vanished. The punishment for stealing was novel and very effectual as a preventive. There was nothing so small that it was not of some value to us there, and if a man was caught stealing he was immediately seized, and one half of his head was shaved, and with a few sound kicks or cuffs, or a few hearty spanks with a shake he was sent adrift in the prison. Very few men chose to incur this punishment a second time, for they were liable to receive punishment of some kind while the mark was on them, wherever they might go. As soon as possible they would get some friend to shave the other side of their head, and thus after a while the mark would wear off.

The current rate of exchange during this period was about three dollars Confederate for one dollar Greenback, and so great was the desire for *gold* with the rebs, that there was practically no limit where gold was offered. A ten-dollar gold piece would probably have brought one thousand dollars in Confederate money, perhaps $10,000. The only one of our party who had any money was John Rapp. He divided with us as long as it lasted, and suffered uncomplainingly with us when it was gone. His eighteen dollars, all he had, procured us many things that we needed, but at fearfully high prices.

A list of prices of food might not be uninteresting in this connection. Onions were from 25 to 75 cents each, eggs 40 cents each, potatoes one dollar per dozen, salt five cents a tablespoonful, beans 40 cents a pint, corn meal 25 cents a quart, honey (wild) five dollars a pound, biscuits 25 cents each, molasses 50 cents a half pint, bacon ten cents a ration, peaches 25 to 75 cents each, and sour beer five cents a cup. The latter drink was made by mixing certain quantities of sorghum, corn meal, and water together, and allowing it to stand in the sun until fermented. I never bought any, because I had no money, but I got some one night as a reward for playing the violin. A friend of mine who was acquainted with a wealthy prisoner (a sort of merchant prince who had a stand on the main street opposite the north gate, and lived in a big board shanty), got permission of him to have me try a violin which he had. He was very careful before allowing me to take the violin, to examine my fingernails to see that they were not so long as to endanger cutting the strings. I won his confidence to such an extent, by my music, that he voluntarily presented me with a doughnut (that was what he called it) and three cups of sour beer, and invited me at the close of the concert to repeat the programme the following evening. There were no bouquets. The doughnut was good, the sour beer was nectar, but the violin was bliss unbounded. I had not seen one for months, and the touch of it was like clasping the hand of a dear friend after a long absence.

Chapter Three

While writing this, the memories of those days, of the brave, noble boys who laid down their lives there, came thronging on me faster than I could commit them to paper. I can see them as they were in those dreadful days, as they would come together to comfort each other with favorable rumors of exchange, or to tell of the passing away of some comrade or of the serious illness of another, and the look of despair and of hopelessness in their faces was the saddest thing I ever saw. I will tax your patience long enough only to make mention of a few.

John Magar of Hyde Park was one, a boy who had fished and hunted and gone chestnutting with me lots of times on the hills back of Hyde Park.[17] I met him soon after I got in prison; he belonged to a New York State regiment. He was a lighthearted boy, but the prison life broke him down soon. I saw him failing day by day and I finally prevailed on him to go out to the hospital. I helped him to the gate one morning and saw him pass out. I never met him again. He got better, I heard, and after I left Andersonville he was taken to Millen [Georgia] prison, was taken sick again, and died there October 10th, 1864.

Alexander Elmendorf was another, a giant in stature and strength and an angel in temper and disposition.[18] He was not fleshy, but would weigh in ordinary conditions 225 pounds, and his strength was so great he hardly knew its extent himself. He boarded with my parents when he enlisted in the Harris Light Cavalry. He was captured in Virginia, escaped from the rebs, and hid in the swamps, I think, for a week or more, until starvation drove him to surrender. He was brought to Andersonville, and when I met him there I hardly knew him. He was shrunken in weight and his shoulders were stooped and the old life and spirit was gone out of him. The coarse and scanty food did not satisfy his cravings and he daily drooped and drooped until we saw that death would soon claim him unless he would have some relief. I helped to carry him to the gate one morning and he also went out to the hospital, but it was too late, and there was but little difference at this time between the hospital and the stockade, and in a short time he too laid down his life for his country.

Samuel Crippen another, a brother of Ben Crippen, the brave color bearer of the 143rd, as brave and true as his brother, but destined as was his brother to fill an unknown grave. I helped him also to the gate and he went out, but it was not to life and liberty as we fondly hoped it would be, but to add one more to the glorious band of patriots who gave their lives that "this government of the people, for the people and by the people, should not perish from the earth."[19]

At last John Hartung, of Honesdale.[20] He belonged to the Pennsylvania Reserves. I had a pocket knife, one of the most valuable articles you could possibly own in prison. (Rapp also had a knife which, made two in our squad.) Johnny had no knife, and I frequently loaned him mine. One day he came to me with a small Bible in his hand and said to me, "Here, you take this and take care of it while I have your knife." Poor fellow, he thought I ought to have some security for my knife, and this was all he had to offer. I was very glad to accept his offer indeed. I had never read the Bible a great deal before and was surprised to find how interesting it was, and how many passages there were which were comforting to us in our forlorn condition. I spent very many hours in the study of this blessed book and became so much attached to it that I made frequent suggestions to Johnny looking to a permanent trade, but somehow he never seemed ready to make it.

At last the time came when they commenced moving us from Andersonville, and it became necessary for me to know which I would take with me, the knife or the Bible. I went to Johnny with the Bible, and told him that as we might have to go at any time, we had better each take our own property. He made the exchange, taking the Bible and giving me the knife, but he was very reluctant to do it. He came over to our place in a short time after with the Bible and, sitting down on the ground alongside of me, said, "I guess I will have to let you have it. My little girl put it in my hands the last thing as I left my home and until I let you have it, it was always in my breast pocket next to my heart, but I cannot do without the knife, and I don't think she would care if she knew how necessary the knife is to me." As he spoke the tears rolled down his cheeks and we cried together. Poor Johnny—he died in Andersonville after we left, with the Bible on his heart and the knife in his pocket.

I could name many more as brave and true as these were, who died there; many who were spared to get home to die, where their last hours were spent in the companionship of those they loved, and very many, who, smitten there, have dropped by the wayside in the years which they have passed since the war. They died as the result of a military policy which doubtless hastened the close of the war and saved many thousand soldiers in the field, but made the prisoners of war the helpless victims of a purpose on the part of the Confederacy which filled more graves from the prisons than were filled on all the battlefields of the war in the same time.

In times of sudden peril the mind of man, whether believer or infidel, instinctively turns to God. The quick, short, heartfelt prayer— God help me—rises to the lips of the sinner as well as the saint, and with equal fervor and earnest desire in times of great danger. But in Andersonville it seemed as if the continued misery, the hunger, and the horrors all about us drew our minds further from God, and His name was seldom heard except as it was taken in vain. We were so full of the misery each man carried in his own soul that there seemed to be no room for the emotions which drew man nearer to his Saviour. There were a few devoted, Godly men, however, who, beginning almost at the opening of the prison, continued unceasingly until its gates swung open for the last time to present to the dying souls there the promises of God and the hope of a blessed eternity with Him. They truly came with the spirit of the Lord upon them, to present the Gospel to the poor (for we were poor) to heal the brokenhearted (were more brokenhearted people ever assembled in any one place?) to preach deliverance to the captives (how we hungered for that), and the recovery of sight to the blind (all morally, many physically so), and to set at liberty them that were bruised. One would think that with all these practical applications many would have sought the Saviour, but it was not so. Of this little band of workers, I only knew one personally, and he was Frank W. Smith of Toledo, Ohio.[21] He is now, or was the last I knew of him, an Evangelist. In his love for God and his fellow man he gave up his chance for exchange to a sick comrade, and remained in Andersonville. It was an act rare and noble, for it was almost signing his own death warrant.

An account of Andersonville would be incomplete that did not record the acts of Father [William] Hamilton, a Roman Catholic Clergyman of Macon, Ga. Day after day he was in the prison speaking words of cheer and comfort to Catholics and Protestants alike, ministering to the dying of his own church, giving a cup of water or a kind word to any suffering soul who might need it, and doing many acts of Christian kindness to those who had come to regard themselves as abandoned almost by God himself.[22]

. . . When we first went into the prison we carefully divided our little pittance each day into three meals, but we found it was too much care to watch and guard our reserve, and we concluded to make two meals of it instead—morning and evening—but for the same reason we were obliged to come down to the regular style and finally we made one meal a day, and that as soon as the rations were drawn, thus avoiding all care and running no risk of being robbed. The stream which supplied us with water came into prison after passing through the rebel camp, and the cook shanties, and was considerably polluted before it reached us. We were forced to dig wells, and these were also polluted by the deposits of filth throughout the camp, the whole surface of which was saturated with excreta. These wells were sunk in some instances to great depths, and I hear that so many of them still remain that it is even now dangerous to travel through the old prison ground without a guide. The ground is of a sandy nature and after getting down a short distance the sand is very compact and does not cave in.[23]

The wells which were sunk near the stockade became convenient means of running tunnels leading outside the stockade. Quite a number of prisoners escaped by these tunnels, but very few succeeded in getting very far from the prison before they were retaken and brought back. The stream and wells were insufficient to supply the

camp, and we were really suffering for water with no prospect of relief, when what may be truly styled a miracle took place. I speak of
what I saw and know to be a fact, and my evidence can be corrobo-
rated by the evidence of thousands even today, so that it does not admit of contradiction. On the evening before it occurred, we were almost wild for water, the stream was filthy, and the wells were worse.
The weather was intensely hot and we were feverish and thirsty, and
with all of our trouble and suffering it seemed as if God had forgotten and forsaken us. It was my custom to get up very early, before the
main camp was astir, and go down to the creek and get a can of water before the rush began. On my way down I noticed two or three
men with tin cups tied on the ends of poles, reaching over the deadline to a spring which clear as crystal had burst from the side hill during the night and was pouring down its precious flood between the
deadline and the stockade. Oh! What joy; God had not forgotten us,
but in the most signal manner had answered the prayers for help
which had been so earnestly made to him. It was very dangerous,
however, fishing for water here, for the least encroachment on the
deadline would bring a death shot from the guard only a few feet
distant on the stockade. The rebels soon came in with a detail and
led the water in troughs to our side of the deadline, where we could
get it without exposing ourselves. Shortly after, a large trough was
placed there in which a dozen pails could be dipped at once and
from that time until the gates of Andersonville opened for the last
time, there was no scarcity of water there.

Several years ago, while visiting Andersonville as one of the [mem-
bers] of the Pennsylvania Monument Commission, I visited the
spring and drank of its cool, refreshing water. The National Women's
Relief Corps Auxiliary to the Grand Army of the Republic has
erected over the spring a beautiful pavilion of Georgia granite. It
does not seem like the spot where the thirsty thousands gathered on
those hot August days, but the volume of water is as strong today as
it was then and as much or more water flows from this spring as
comes into the prison ground by the stream.[24]

During the night of August 9th, a severe thunderstorm visited us
and several [lightning] bolts in the course of the storm struck in or
near the prison. It was said that one of these bolts struck an old pine
stump, and as the spring burst forth from the foot of this stump that

Breaking out of Providence Spring

it was the result of the lightning stroke. Possibly God may have chosen to bring the water by this agency. All the same, whether by this or the word of His power, He brought it and that was enough for us.

Our diet being almost entirely vegetable and being varied but very little, brought to us sooner or later the scurvy. The quantity and quality, and variety of rations was better if anything in Andersonville than in Florence. We had meat oftener, and a little larger ration of all kinds than we had in Florence. But it was not enough to support life at the best. Our daily rations at this time were, if cooked, a piece of corn bread about two inches thick, two and a half inches wide, and six inches long, sometimes a small piece of bacon about one and a half inches square, or three ounces of boiled beef. Sometimes we would get boiled rice, about a pint, or boiled beans, same quantity. The bacon was the only thing that was at all salt, the bread, rice, and beans were cooked without salt. The beans, as we called them, were the little red cowpeas raised all through the Carolinas and Georgia for the cattle. They are very nutritious and we all preferred them to any other rations issued to us. You probably would not relish them as we did if they were given to you as we got them. Any of you who have ever prepared peas for planting in the spring of the year have no doubt noticed a little black bug which seems to have his home in the pea. Almost every one of these peas had such a tenant, and the bug and the pea went into the soup together. Now, it may appear strange to you, but it is nevertheless a fact, we did not pick out and throw away the bugs. If we had done so, there would have been mighty little of the pea left. We were not particular about a bug or two, more or less.

We did not get salt every day, occasionally a teaspoonful was issued each man. If we drew uncooked rations, it would be about a pint of coarsely ground meal, a great deal of cob being left in it, or a little less than a half pint of rice or beans, sometimes a ration of bacon or beef. We never got the rice, the corn, or meal and the beans at the same time, only one of the three. The question with us was how to cook what we got, to make it go farthest. Our ration of wood was very scanty, so small that it was not possible to cook a ration of either beans, rice, or corn meal with it. It was only by clubbing two or three rations of wood together that we could thoroughly cook these things. When we drew raw fresh beef we were in great luck and there was great joy when a marrow bone was drawn. That would add richness to the beans or rice equal to green turtle, and afterwards would make rings and trinkets to sell to the rebs. We did not attempt to cook the raw meat. The heat of the sun was so great that we used it to do the cooking. By laying the beef on top of the rubber blankets in the sun, in about an hour it would be very good dried beef. It was very necessary, however, to stand right by and superintend the drying. Out of the corn meal, we made mush, mostly very thin mush, sometimes corn meal balls, but these only when the rations were larger than usual. Our mess did not draw uncooked rations very often, as we had very few things to cook in.

The older prisoners preferred the uncooked rations, as they could make them go farther, and they could do more trading with them. Immediately after the rations had been issued each day, all over the prison would be heard the cry of the traders, "Who will trade a ration of meat for a plug of tobacco? Who will trade a ration of salt for a marrow bone?" (The marrow was likely to be out of the bone,

however, by this time.) "Who will buy a ration of beans? Who will
trade a ration of meal for a ration of bacon?" and so on.

I have made mention frequently of tents, but there was not a tent
in the prison. What I mean by that is the shelters we had to protect
us from the sun. These shelters were made from various articles—
shirts and drawers ripped apart, old bags, and even coats and pants.
Of course the shelter afforded was of the most scanty kind, but shelter of some kind was absolutely necessary to the preservation of life.

It is remarkable to what degree hunger will blunt the most acute
senses. No one could have been more sensitive to anything offensive
in smell or taste than myself, but so much did my hunger overcome
my taste or smell or both, that I have drawn and eaten cooked meat
which was in the first stages of decay, without the least desire or inclination to divide it with anyone else. It did not taste as well as good
meat would, and left a burning sensation in my throat, but I suffered
no ill effects from it. Almost every prisoner who had been in two
months had the scurvy. I had been in about three months before it
appeared on me.

In referring to the exchanges of currency in the stockade, I omit-
ted mention of two very important articles which were current as currency, and which were next in order of demand to Greenbacks, viz;
buttons and peppers. A general opinion had gained ground that peppers and sweet potatoes were the best remedies for scurvy we could
get, and of course there was a great demand for them, the peppers
especially, as a little pepper would go a great way. When money and
trinkets of various kinds were exhausted, we had to fall back on something else as a purchasing power. Luckily for us we had buttons, and
buttons were in great demand among the rebs. I do not know what
the Confederate Army regulations were with regard to buttons, but
I do know that there seemed to be no limit to the number a reb
would put on his coat if he had them. The buttons were of several
grades in value, the lowest being the regulation button, the next the
New York State button, and the highest the Officers and Staff buttons. An ordinary button would buy from one to a dozen peppers, a
New York State button much more, while a Staff button would corner the pepper market. I have seen private reb soldiers with four rows
of buttons in front and a corresponding number on cuffs and coat-
tails. When a pepper merchant came in prison, the boys would flock

around him in great numbers, and the chances were, unless he was very careful, he would lose as many buttons as he bought, for the boys engaging him in front bargaining for peppers would give opportunity to their friends behind, to cut the buttons from the tail of his coat.

Most of the rebel soldiers with whom we came in contact were simpleminded men, with an inordinate desire to possess some article of Yankee manufacture, knife, tool, bone-ring, or charm, and they would pay good prices for them in the currency of the camp. The Home Guards or Georgia Reserves, who were among those guarding us, were young country fellows principally, who had never been to the front, and had never seen much of the world and almost everything was curious and interesting to them.[25] They had much less regard for human life than the old soldiers who had seen service, and most of our boys who were killed at the deadline were killed by the young boys. The feeling of the old reb soldiers for the Home Guards

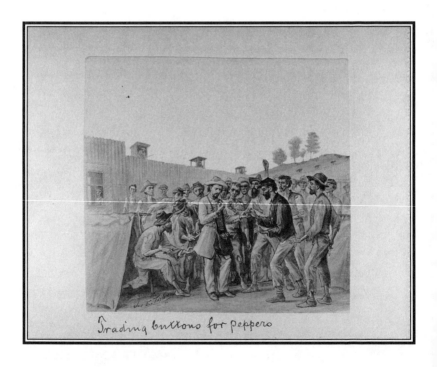

Trading buttons for peppers

or Reserves was not very cordial. The old soldiers felt a contempt for them and never called them by any other name than the "Georgia Preserves."

I have never said a word against the bravery and good fighting qualities of the Southern soldier. To discredit these qualities in them would be to discredit them in ourselves, for we are of one race and one people and I think one has no advantage of the other, but I think in the mass, the Northern soldier was more intelligent, better educated, and less disposed to be cruel. The curse of slavery was to blame largely for this in the Southerner. I do not, however, hold the rank and file responsible for the cruelties practiced upon us. They are traceable to a higher source. The men who could appoint such a cruel, bloodthirsty monster as General John W. Winder to the supreme command of all the prisons in the South have gone to answer to a just God for that act, and its consequences.[26]

Several instances will illustrate the character of General Winder. When remonstrated with by an Inspector, who came to inspect Andersonville, against the crowded condition of the prison, and was asked to at least give the prisoners more room, he answered that he proposed to let them stay just as they were, the operations of death would soon clean out the crowd, so that survivors would have plenty of room. And again he made the heartless boast that he was killing off more Yankees than twenty regiments of Lee's Army. General Winder remained in command of the Confederate prisons until his death which occurred . . . [February 8,] 1865, at Florence, S.C., where God, seeing his iniquity was full, struck him down without a moment's warning. Of the character of this man and the fact that his coldblooded, murderous acts were known to his superiors and approved by them, let me give you some evidence from rebel sources. This evidence is part of the Government record and is indisputable. Humanity was not entirely dead in the South and the reports of the cruelties being practiced on the prisoners in Andersonville coming so numerously and continuously from all sources the rebel Government was forced in spite of itself to take notice of them, and finally sent Col. D. T. Chandler of the War Department to Andersonville to make an inspection of the prison. Under date of August 5th, 1864, he sends his report and the following is an extract from it:

My duty requires me respectfully to recommend a change in the Officer in command of the Post, Brigadier Gen. John H. Winder, and the substitution in his place of some one who unites both energy and good judgment with some feelings of *humanity* and consideration for the welfare and comfort, as far as is consistent with their safe keeping, of the vast number of unfortunates placed under his control. Some one who at least, will not advocate *deliberately* and in cold blood, the propriety of leaving them in their present condition until their number is sufficiently reduced to make the present arrangements suffice for their accommodation, and who will not consider it a self laudation and boasting that he has never been inside of the stockade a place the horrors of which it is difficult to describe, and which is a disgrace to civilization—the condition of which he might by the exercise of a little energy and judgment, even with the limited means at his command have considerably improved.

Afterwards, when called to a further examination concerning his report, Col. Chandler testified:

I noticed that General Winder seemed very indifferent to the welfare of the prisoners, indisposed to do anything or to do as much as I thought he ought to do, to alleviate their suffering. I remonstrated with him as well as I could, and he used that language which I reported to the Department with reference to it—the language stated in the report. When I spoke of the great mortality existing among the prisoners, and pointed out to him that the sickly season was coming on, and that it must necessarily increase unless something was done for their relief—the swamp for instance drained, proper food furnished and in better quantity, and other sanitary suggestions which I made to him—he replied to me that he thought it was better to see half of them die than to take care of them.

In the face of this damning testimony Winder was retained in his position and carried out his purposes —and the purposes of the Confederate Government to the last.[27]

In July 1864, it was reported that several expeditions had been started from our lines to liberate us. The artillery of the prison was so placed that every foot of the inside of the prison could be swept by a battery of twenty-five guns. When word came to Winder that such expeditions were planned he issued the following order:

Head Quarters Military Prison
Andersonville, Ga., July 27th, 1864

Order No. 13.

The officers on duty and in charge of the Battery of Florida Artillery at the time, will, upon receiving notice that the enemy has approached within seven miles of this post, open upon the stockade with grape-shot, without reference to the situation beyond these lines of defense.

(Signed) John H. Winder
Brig. Gen. Commanding.

Thirty thousand prisoners, helpless, many sick, many dying, unable to take any offensive part themselves, to be opened upon with grapeshot at close range because there was danger that they might be liberated. Does history record anything more devilish? This was not war, it was hellish hatred seeking the chance to commit murder.

Although he was not allowed to carry out his plans in this case, he was not entirely foiled of his purpose. Before the first day of the following April he succeeded so far as to have buried of those who were confined in Andersonville alone, nearly 13,000 prisoners. It is over 40 years ago that all this happened. If you could see that prison as I have seen it, if you could feel the tortures of thirst, heat, hunger, and disease, as we felt them, if you could know a tithe of the horrors of that hell as we knew them, I think you would excuse my inability and the inability of all or any who endured it, to forget and forgive the most foul and horrible act that ever stained the history of a Christian nation.

In the meantime, forces were at work which were going to release us from Andersonville, but not from captivity. Sherman was thundering at Atlanta and was soon to take up the march to the sea. The

Confederacy began to consider the expediency of moving us out of the possible track of his operations, and we began to hear rumors of exchange. The rebs always started such rumors before moving us as it had the effect of keeping us more quiet and there was less liability of our trying to escape en route. At last it was announced as a fact that we were to be taken out as rapidly as possible to Charleston and there exchanged, as a fleet of vessels loaded with reb prisoners were there waiting for us. This had its effect and all were anxious to go. We were taken out by detachments, the first on the 8th of September. On the 13th of September in the evening just as our rations for the day had been brought in, the order was given for our detachment to fall in and take the cars. The line formed very quickly and many forgot their hunger in their anxiety to get out. I did not. We had boiled rice that night and it was smoking hot. I filled my haversack as full as it would hold and with both hands as full as I could hold them of the hot rice, I fell in at the tail end of the detachment as it filed out of the south gate of Andersonville, and took up the march for the cars which were to convey us, as we hoped, to liberty.

We passed through Macon, Georgia, on the 15th, through Augusta on the 16th, and arrived at Charleston on the 17th and were marched to the race course, where we went into camp and were surrounded by a double line of guards. It was well for me I had taken the rice, for the rebs failed to issue any rations and we suffered greatly for food until the night of the 17th. While lying at the race course we could see the shells from our batteries on Morris Island coming over the city and exploding, and we could not help once in a while giving a faint cheer, but it didn't sound like a cheer any more than the voice of a child resembles that of a full-grown man. The second day after, they called for volunteers to go to someplace up in the country, and feeling certain there was no hope for exchange and being anxious to be on the go, I volunteered along with some 1,500 others and formed the first lot of prisoners who were taken to Florence, South Carolina, a prison which holds in its boundaries today, the bodies of 2,800 Union prisoners who gave up their lives there between the 17th day of September, 1864, and the last of February, 1865.

Of Andersonville, Miss Evelyn Greay Lambert, of South Bend, Indiana, after a visit to the site of the prison, has written as follows:

Peaceful and quiet now the place,
The careless traveler finds small trace
            Of scenes enacted here.
And yet, so full of memories dread.
It seems as if the very dead,
Among whose graves the living tread,
            Might waken, and appear,
When'er the ill-famed name is breathed,
And tell of tortures worse than death.

Full thirty thousand loyal men
Were crowded in that loathsome pen,
            In wretched misery;
All shelterless, with scanty food,
Deprived of all things bright and good,
E'en the poor boon of solitude
            Denied, and each must see
His comrade's wan and wasted face
Where famine left its deadly trace.

And, like the Inquisitors of old,
To all of mercy's pleading cold
            Were those who held them there,
Where days and nights were constant pain
Till souls were sick and minds were slain,
And madness passed from brain to brain
            Contagious on the air;
Till they whose reason held its throne
Feared this dark fate would be their own.

And yet those heroes, faithful, true,
No thought of change or turning knew,
            Loyal their every breath;
The ghastly lines of graves grew long,
Proved their devotion pure and strong;
They would not their country wrong,
            E'en to escape from death;

And, scorning death, despising pain,
Their honor kept without a stain.

But soldiers now possess the ground
That made the gloomy prison's bound
*   To hold, a sacred trust.*
Then guard it well, O, comrades mine,
And keep the spot a pilgrim shrine,
Where patriots may their offering twine
*   O'er mounds of precious dust,*
Where hero-martyrs silent sleep
Their last, long slumber calm and deep.

And give the praise, so nobly earned
By faithfulness that never turned
*   From duty's hardest ways;*
For nameless graves the truth proclaim,
Their lives were given not for fame
Nor hope on history's page to claim
*   A word of deathless praise;*
But patriot love for native land
Inspired endurance brave and grand.

Notes

Chapter 1

1. Colonel Henry M. Hoyt was promoted to brigadier general in 1865. After the war he was elected governor of Pennsylvania. Lieutenant Colonel John B. Conyngham also survived his wounds and was mustered out with the regiment on July 12, 1865. First Lieutenant Silas Bunyan, originally of Company D, died of his wounds in Charleston, S.C., on July 3, 1864. Bates, *History of Penn. Volunteers* (Volume 3; pp.61, 74.)

2. Private John A. Rapp, a farmer by occupation, joined for duty and enrolled on January 3, 1862, at Reading, Pa. He was mustered into Company K, 52nd Pennsylvania, on January 14, 1862, at Harrisburg. He reenlisted as a veteran volunteer on January 1, 1864. By then he had turned twenty years of age. Rapp was captured at James Island on July 3, 1864, released from captivity on November 30, 1864, and was discharged from the service on January 14, 1865. Service Record.

3. Michael Beavers, originally of Oxford, New Jersey, enlisted as a private in Company K, 52nd Pennsylvania Volunteer Infantry, on January 29, 1862. He was five feet eight inches tall with gray eyes and black hair. Beavers was forty-one years of age at the time of his enlistment. He was paroled on December 13, 1864, at Charleston, S.C., and mustered out of the Union army on June 21, 1865. Service Record.

4. According to his service record in the National Archives, John Brennan did not enlist until February 20, 1865. Apparently, however, there were two John Brennans. Bates's *History of the Pennsylvania Volunteers* shows Brennan enlisting on January 24, 1862, and mustering out on March 6, 1865.

5. This was Private William *Goodwin*, formerly of New York City, who was drafted and mustered in on July 20, 1863, in Philadelphia. A common laborer by occupation, Goodwin was twenty-five years old at the time he was drafted. He was five feet eight and a quarter inches tall with black eyes, dark hair, and a dark complexion. He "died in

rebel prison at Florence, S.C. on or about November 15, 1864. Cause of death not known." Service Record.

6. Edward L. Dana was mustered in to the 143rd Pennsylvania Volunteer Infantry as the colonel of the regiment on November 18, 1862. He was exchanged shortly after his capture and was ordered to rejoin his regiment on August 23, 1864. He was retroactively promoted to brigadier general on June 22, 1867, with an effective date of July 26, 1865. Dana was mustered out on August 4, 1865. Service Record.

7. The 5th Georgia Infantry was organized in May 1861 with an initial strength of 825 soldiers. Its men came from Camden, Clinch, Dawson, McDuffie, Schley, Spalding, and Upson counties, Georgia. By the time Ripple had arrived in Andersonville, the 5th had participated in the battles of Murfreesboro, Chickamauga, and Chattanooga. The 55th Georgia Infantry organized in August 1862 with a beginning strength of 1,008 and was comprised of men who came primarily from the Georgia counties of Jackson, Walker, and Hall. Much of the regiment had been captured at Cumberland Gap, Tennessee, on September 10, 1863. After the soldiers were exchanged, the regiment performed guard duty in Georgia and the Carolinas. *The American Civil War Regimental Informational System* (Software); Vol. I (Albuquerque, 1994).

8. This was normally the case, with the exception that white officers of black regiments were not recognized to be "real" officers by the Confederates; instead they were considered to be leaders of slave insurrectionists. As such, these officers were confined at enlisted men's prisons, such as Andersonville.

9. Leander Overpeck enlisted as a corporal in Company F, 52nd Pennsylvania Infantry, on September 19, 1861, when he was twenty-one years old. He was paroled on February 22, 1865. He was mustered out on March 1, 1865. Service Record. Corporal Samuel Smith joined for duty and enrolled on August 22, 1861, at Scranton, Pennsylvania. He mustered into the 52nd at Pottsville, Pennsylvania, on September 23, 1861, for three years. His records indicate he was twenty-two years of age, but it is not clear if he was that age when he enlisted or if he was twenty-two when he was discharged in 1865. Service Record.

Chapter 2

10. Ripple underestimated the number of prisoners. By this time Andersonville had about 30,000 inmates.

11. In the later version of his memoirs, Ripple included at this point a page of statistics concerning deaths, burials, percentage of deaths, escapes, hospitalizations, etc., gleaned from *Official Records of the War of the Rebellion.*

12. Ripple overestimated a bit. The largest number of prisoners held in Andersonville Prison totaled just over 32,000 in August 1864.

13. At five feet six inches with light hair, blue eyes, and a florid complexion, twenty-four-year-old Perry H. Fuller enlisted at Easton, Pennsylvania on February 27, 1864, as a private in Battery C, of the Provisional 2nd Regiment, Pennsylvania Heavy Artillery, for three years service. Born in Susquehanna County, Pennsylvania, he was a painter by occupation. Service Record.

14. These soldiers most likely were members of Company K, 1st Michigan Sharpshooters. Company K was comprised, among others, of Chippewas and Ottawas. Ted Alexander, "Native American in the Civil War" (1993). Unpublished National Park Service report, Antietam National Battlefield, Sharpsburg, Maryland.

15. In addition to the hangings, several of the Raiders received lesser punishments, such as wearing balls and chains or being strung up by the thumbs. The six Raiders sentenced to death were Patrick Delaney and William Collins of Pennsylvania, Charles Curtis of Rhode Island, John Sarsfield of New York, and A. Munn of the U.S. Navy. There is some confusion as to the real name of the sixth Raider who was hanged. Although his tombstone is inscribed "W. Rickson U.S.N.," research indicates that his real name was Sullivan. See Ovid L. Futch, *History of Andersonville Prison* (Gainesville, Florida: University of Florida Press, 1968); p.71 (footnote).

16. Private Ivory Emory, Company F, 1st Regiment Massachusetts Heavy Artillery, had been a bootmaker prior to his enlistment at the age of thirty-five on November 28, 1863. He stood five feet four inches tall and had hazel eyes, brown hair, and a dark complexion. He was captured near Petersburg, Virginia, on June 22, 1864. Emory died of the disease on August 14, 1864, and is buried in grave No. 5619, Andersonville National Cemetery. Service Record.

Chapter 3

17. No record of John Magar could be found.

18. Alexander Elmendorf enlisted in Captain Dunscomb's Company of the Harris Light Cavalry (later Company K, 2nd New York Cavalry) on August 21, 1861, at the age of twenty-five. During his service he spent much of his time as a teamster, cook, and "axeman." Elmendorf was captured at Reams Station, Virginia, on July 5, 1864. His POW record states that he "died from diaharea *[sic]*" in the Andersonville Hospital some time after August 4, 1864. Service Record.

19. No record of Samuel Crippen could be found. Sergeant Benjamin Crippen was killed on July 1, 1863, at Gettysburg. He is depicted on the 143rd Pennsylvania Infantry monument on that battlefield, waving his fist defiantly at the oncoming Confederates while clasping the flag in his other hand.

20. No record of John Hartung of the Pennsylvania Reserves could be found. There was a John Hartung in the 107th Pennsylvania Infantry, but he was not captured until December 8, 1864, and he survived to be mustered out on June 7, 1865. Service Record.

21. First Sergeant Frank W. Smith, Company D, 124th Regiment Ohio Infantry, enlisted on February 4, 1864, in Cleveland after previously serving in Company E, 84th Ohio Infantry. When he was wounded and captured near Dallas, Georgia, on May 24, 1864, he was twenty-two years old. Smith was five feet ten inches, had blue eyes, brown hair, and a dark complexion. His civilian occupation was listed as "clerk." He was paroled on March 5, 1865, and was discharged on June 7, 1865. Service Record.

22. When Father Hamilton returned to his pastorate in Macon, he corresponded with his bishop to inform him of the need for more clergy at Andersonville Prison. The bishop responded by directing three Georgia priests to Camp Sumter to minister to the prisoners. William Marvel, *Andersonville: The Last Depot* (Chapel Hill, N.C.: University of North Carolina Press, 1994); p.140.

23. Prior to this paragraph (in the bound, typed version of his memoirs), Ripple again cites some statistics—this time comparing Union battle losses to prison deaths—quoted from another book on Andersonville by a contemporary of Ripple's, John McElroy, who

wrote *Andersonville: A Story of a Rebel Military Prison* (Toledo: D. R. Locke, 1879).

24. Today visitors can still drink from the spring by means of a drinking faucet.

25. The Georgia Reserves was a form of militia unit authorized for state defense. It was comprised primarily of men in their late forties and teenagers. See Marvel, *Andersonville;* pp.62–63.

26. General John Henry Winder had been the provost marshal and prison commandant in Richmond early in the war. In June 1864 he was given responsibility for Andersonville Prison (since the prisoners were transferred there from the Belle Isle Prison in Richmond) and in November he was given responsibility for all his prisons east of the Mississippi River. He died before the end of the war on February 8, 1865. Had he survived, he most likely would have been tried and executed as a war criminal. Patricia L. Faust, ed., *Historical Times Illustrated Encyclopedia of the Civil War* (New York: Harper and Row, 1985), p.836.

27. In the typed, bound version of his memoirs, Ripple includes another Chandler report, along with endorsements from other officers in Chandler's chain-of-command, as further evidence that the Confederate authorities were not only aware of the conditions at Andersonville, they were appalled by it. These reports appear in the *Official Records,* Series 2, Volume VII. Apparently, animosity existed between Chandler and Winder, so that these reports may not be entirely accurate. One of the early professional historians to write about Andersonville was William B. Hesseltine. According to this scholar, "Writers of prison reminiscences cite this report as evidence of the cruelty of their captors. Winder denied Chandler's statements, although he did not know the opinion which Chandler had expressed as to the fitness for his office. The matter became a question of the truthfulness of the two officers and a military court was ordered to settle the matter. The death of Winder and the end of the war prevented this court from meeting." Hesseltine, *Civil War Prisons: A Study in War Psychology* (Columbus: Ohio State University Press, 1930 [repub. by Frederick Ungar Pub. Co., New York, 1964]), p.149 (fn 68).

PART II
Florence

Chapter Four

When Andersonville was selected as a prison depot, it seemed secure by its isolated position from any visitation by our troops as long as the war would last. But when the campaign of 1864 fairly opened and Grant in Virginia and Sherman in Georgia began to press them at all points, a pressure which ended only at the grave of the Confederacy, the rebel authorities began to see that ere the summer would pass away, Andersonville, instead of being in the heart of the Confederacy, would be dangerously near the edge.

In the latter part of June, Gen. Stoneman with a strong body of troops started from Sherman's army on a raid inside the rebel lines, having for one of its objects the liberation of the prisoners at Andersonville. The raid was a failure and resulted in the defeat and dispersion of the force with the capture of many of the raiders.[1] It was this raid which occasioned the infamous order of Gen. Winder, the Commandant of all the rebel prisons, in which he directed the officers in charge of the Battery of Florida Artillery, on the approach of our troops within seven miles of the prison, to open on the stockade with grapeshot. The excuse given for the issuance of such an order, being that these prisoners let loose on the Confederacy, would commit unheard of atrocities. Before Gen. Winder, a self-constituted court, we were accused, tried, adjudged guilty, and sentenced to death before having committed any offense. The fact is, it was a blessing that the raid was a failure. If successful, the result would have been disastrous in the extreme unless the raiding force had been strong enough to have maintained its position against any force the enemy could bring, while supplying itself and the prisoners with food, or to have retraced its way to our lines with its convoy of sick and enfeebled prisoners. Either case would have been next to an impossibility and the result would have been the death by neglect and starvation of thousands within a few days, for in all that host of prisoners not one-fourth would have borne arms and done duty in the field, while the other three-fourths were in all stages of disease and helplessness, the most of whom could not have sustained the fatigue of a march of five miles a day.

The dead and dying and sick would have had to be abandoned to save the others, and that would never have been considered for a moment. The severe blows being dealt the enemy by Grant and Sherman required all their attention and all the force at their command. No one point could be depleted to help another, for all points found themselves too weak to withstand the terrible hammering they were getting. All able-bodied men were hurried to the front and to the Georgia Reserves . . . was assigned the task of guarding the prisoners. The cradle and the grave had truly been robbed to form this body of troops, and they were the last possible draft of the Confederacy. They were composed of the siftings of all the conscriptions which had been levied on the South, boys of 16 to 18, and old men from 60 years and over. There were some few Union men among them who were induced to take service by that most moving and convincing argument—a line of bayonets in the rear.

If we could have had our choice, we would have a thousand times preferred to be guarded by the men we had been battling with on the line of battle or skirmish line than by men who had never been under fire. There is that experience in war which will make a good soldier respect a brave and stubborn enemy, and when the fortunes of war have thrown him into his hands will treat him as kindly and considerately as his duties or circumstances will permit. It was not so, however, with the skulkers, the cowards, and the inconsiderate youth who made up this body of troops. They had not faced the fire of an enemy and had not learned to respect him, and they sought to establish a reputation for bravery by assuming towards helpless prisoners the ferocity and cruelty of wild beasts. The rebel authorities, knowing their inability to guard this large body of prisoners with the troops at their command, and fearing that they might lose them altogether as the lines were tightening about them, began to look around for other points more inaccessible to our troops and more advantageously located for supplies. Two points in particular were selected, one at Millen, Ga., the other at Florence, S.C.

I cannot say much about Millen, as I was never there. I have, however, heard that the Commandant of that prison was a humane man and that the prisoners suffered less there than in the other prisons. Of Florence I can speak from personal knowledge, as I will farther on.

On the 8th of September, the work of removing the prisoners from Andersonville commenced. The most plausible stories of exchange had previously been circulated through the prison by the rebel guards, and all were anxious to go. No previous notice was given in order that a detachment would be ready when called out. No notice was necessary. We were not burdened with worldly goods, and we were not so attached to our surroundings that we hesitated to leave

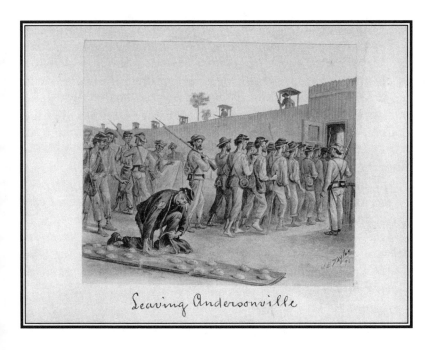

Leaving Andersonville

them. There were no tents to strike, no wagon trains to pack, no lines to form. The rebel sergeant of a detachment would come in and order his detachment to fall in. Inside of ten minutes that detachment would be in line and in ten minutes more it would be on the march. Day after day the exodus continued. On the evening of the 13th day of September . . . the order came for our detachment.

We were crowded into box cars as many as could find standing room in each of the cars, the center being reserved for the guards. . . . During the day in the cars we suffered considerably from the heat and the crowding, but during the night the hardship and suffering were intense. We were crowded together in all stages of sickness and health. All the air we could get was the little that could come in the partly opened door where the guards stood. There were no windows in the car, no ventilation, no seats, no conveniences of any kind. It was standing room only during the day, but we could not stand all night, and there was no room to lie down. Then the heat was intense and the air was so foul it was poison to breathe it. With it all, the road was so rough that we were jostled and shook around, and thrown on each other like ten pins in a bowling alley. Those who made the trip will never forget it.

These changes from one prison to another involving several days and nights on the cars were very hard on us. Like a wounded deer escaping from the hunters and leaving in its track the trail of its life blood, so every passage from prison to prison was marked by the trail of dead behind us. Wherever we went the angel of death was every hour busy in our ranks. All along the lines which carried us from Andersonville to Charleston, to Florence, to Millen, to Blackshear, to Savannah, to Wilmington—the ghastly record marked our passage.

On arriving in Charleston, those who were able to march were formed in column and marched to the Race Course back of the City, and a double line of guards thrown around us. We were wild with hunger, and suffered greatly until the next morning after our arrival, when some hard-tack was distributed among us. During the day a furrow was ploughed around our camp and we were notified that it was the deadline. Some of our boys ran the guard the first night and got away, but were eventually recaptured. The second night the guards were strengthened, and there was no more running the guard.

Irish Woman spilling the milk

While we were lying here, an Irish woman came to the guard line with a pail of milk and asked permission to give it to us. The guard refused her, saying it was against orders. She pleaded and argued with him for a long time to no purpose, while we waited anxiously, hoping she might overcome his scruples. She began to get mad at last and commenced scolding him, but it had no better effect. He finally proposed to her to let him have the milk himself. This seemed to anger her still more, and finding she could not get permission to pass the milk through the lines to us, and determined that the guard, should not have it, she dashed the milk on the ground in front of the guard saying, "If they can't have it, that wants it so badly, the devil a taste shall you have of it, any way." There is no use crying over spilt milk, but we came mighty near doing it that day. As for the guard, he didn't cry, he merely made a few remarks, of a *cursery* nature.

On the second day after our arrival, when we had all become pretty well assured of the fact that there was no prospect of a parole or exchange, we began to discuss among ourselves what the next move would be. We knew this was only a temporary stopping place, as no stockade had yet been built and no arrangements made for our accommodation, so that we were anxious to get away from here as soon as possible. We had frequent evidences that our boys were still on Morris Island in Charleston Harbor, for we could see the shells come over the city and explode and some came quite near to our camp. The distance from us to our forts in the harbor must have been at least seven miles. We could learn nothing whatever of the progress of the war at other points except as some rebel would volunteer some information, and that we knew, of course, must be untrue or he wouldn't tell us.

At this juncture, the choice was given those who desired to, to the number of 1,500, to go to a new camp up the country. Our party volunteered at once to go, and that evening we were marched to the cars and started to Florence, S.C. We were the first arrivals at this place and when we got there were camped out in the field, as no stockade had yet been built. A line of guards was thrown around us and we were told to make ourselves as comfortable as we could. We, our mess, managed to get a pitch pine plank out of a mill pond near by, which was a great find. The plank had been in the pond probably a number of years, but so rich was it in pitch that the water could make no impression on it. We cooked our supper with it and then cut it up in small pieces and stored it up for future use. While lying out in the field we were treated more kindly by the rebels than at any other time during our imprisonment.

Quite a number of the boys got through the guard lines and escaped, but they were all brought back in due time. Some few were gone a week or two and when they were recaptured and brought in, regaled us with stories of how well they lived while they were gone.

The prison stockade was located in the pine woods, and like Andersonville, a stream of water ran through the center, and again like Andersonville, on either side of the stream for some distance there was a swamp. The stockade instead of being built of squared logs as at Andersonville, was built of natural logs set on end 12 feet above the ground, and on the outside an embankment was thrown up sufficiently high to enable the sentries to walk their beats on top of it, thus enabling them to overlook the prison, a much better arrangement than at Andersonville. A large force of slaves were brought from the surrounding country and set to work on the stockade. We enjoyed hearing them sing while they worked. Under the leadership of some *one* they would sing all day and improvise words and music as they went along. They seemed quite happy and worked steadily and well. I afterwards became quite well acquainted with some of them and found them well posted on the subject of the war and what it meant to them. While we were lying out in the fields, we were visited by very many white people from the surrounding country. When allowed by the guards they would talk very freely with us about the war. The argument very seldom varied from the following: "What did you uns come down here to fight we uns for?" We might answer that we were obliged to come out to fight to save the Union. It made little difference, however, what the answer would be, they would invariably come at us with "If you uns had stayed up home and let our niggers alone, we uns wouldn't have gone up there to fight you uns."

They were always anxious to trade with us. Some of our boys had money and they would buy apples and other things of them that the sutler did not have. One day a rebel came up to the line close to where I was, with a meal sack in his hand in which were a dozen apples, little, sour, wormy things that would hardly be fed to the pigs up here. One of the boys bought the apples for $2.00 and paid for them, but as he could not carry them loose, asked the reb to let him carry them in the bag to his tent; he would be back in a minute. The reb instantly consented and he took with him the apples and the bag. He was lost in the crowd before he had gone fifty yards. The reb waited and waited for him but he did not return; the guards would not let him through the lines and he was in great trouble. He had been deceived; the fellow never had intended coming back and he never did come back. Bags were a very valuable commodity. A good bag was worth $25.00. It was good for almost everything. It would make a good shelter and it would make an excellent shirt. All that was required to make a shirt of a sack was to turn the bag closed end up, rip the seam in the middle of the bottom for the head to go through, and rip the seams for the arms on each side of the bag and the shirt was made. The sleeves were "décolleté," and the collar was low cut, but it would answer every purpose.

A meal sack shirt

The most endurable time of my imprisonment was that embraced in the two weeks spent at Florence previous to our going inside the stockade. It was in the early fall and was neither extremely hot nor extremely cold. We got a more generous supply of rations and wood than we had ever had before. The guards were kinder to us and we had a chance to see something beyond the walls of the stockade. But it was too good to last long and the change came when on the second day of October, 1864, we were all ordered to fall in, were counted off, and marched inside the stockade. We were among the first to enter, and having first choice of location, we selected a place in the north corner of the stockade. All the limbs and brush and some of the timber which had been felled had been left on the ground and we were not slow in appropriating a good supply of it.

As the winter was approaching and clothing and covering were scarce with us, we decided that we could shelter ourselves to better advantage if we were divided up into smaller squads, so Brennan, Beavers, Rapp, and I concluded to stay together. Sammy Smith, Davie

Davis, and Nelson Evelands made a mess by themselves.[2] We proceeded at once to gather the limbs and brush and build ourselves huts. We made fireplaces in them and chimneys by mixing clay and making bricks which we dried in the sun. We gathered all the wood we could lay hands on and very soon we began to feel ourselves very rich. We were very comfortably fixed indeed and we felt sorry for the poor fellows who were being brought in each day by train loads from Andersonville, Blackshear, and other prisons, but we were not sorry enough to spare any of our wood for them. As people who feel themselves wealthy and comfortably fixed will sometimes look down a little on those who are not so fortunate, we in our great good fortune could not help indulging a little feeling of that kind towards our poorer comrades. When from the inside of our comfortable huts on a wet or cold day we could lie back and squander two or three ordinary rations of wood on a steady fire all day, and look outside on the poor fellows standing shivering around, we felt that it was a miserable thing to be poor and we congratulated ourselves on our good fortune. As it often happens in this world, there came reverses of fortune, and there was one waiting for us just a little farther on. The place which we had pre-empted happened to be just where the rebels concluded after a few days they wanted to locate the hospital, and one morning right after roll call we (our thousand) were ordered to fall in and be prepared to move to the other side of the creek. What a disappointment this was. We could not move our huts and indeed only so much of our wood as could be carried in our arms, and our nice comfortable houses were lost to us forever.

Poor Davie Davis was one of the first of our boys to sicken after we got inside the stockade.[3] One morning Sammy Smith told me that Davie had gone over to the gate to try to get into the hospital as he was feeling very badly and did not feel able even to get out and answer roll call. As he did not come back that day, I took it for granted he had been successful. In a day or two someone brought me word that one of our boys in the hospital was very low and wanted to see me before he would die. I went over immediately and found it was Davie. I could not get inside the hospital and so was compelled to carry on my conversation with him between cracks or intervals between the boughs and logs of which the hospital was built. He knew that he was going to die and gave me messages for his family and as a last thing gave me his knife. Prisoners of war died in a very matter-of-fact way, there was no struggle, no regrets, no fears. We had had so much suffering in those terrible places that the change was looked forward to in many cases with pleasant anticipations. God knows how far our sins had been cancelled in the suffering. After I got outside of prison and had access to the prison death record, I found the record of Davie's death and with it on my return home furnished the evidence necessary to procure his number in the cemetery and cause of death.[4]

On our arrival at Florence, we were divided into differently numbered detachments from what had been the custom in Andersonville. In Florence, we were divided in thousands first, and then for convenience in counting and distributing the rations, subdivided into hundreds. We were in the first thousand, but I have forgotten what hundred. We were marched over to the southern corner of the stockade and told to take care of ourselves. All the wood had been gathered up; there was not a particle of brush or boughs and nothing of which to construct huts. The summer was gone and the nights were getting cool. The rainy days were already at hand, our clothing was getting fearfully thin, where any of it was left, and we must get someplace to shelter ourselves and to keep warm if possible. We had only our two gum blankets and they were very much worn by this time, but they would do tolerably well to shed water, and would serve to break some of the force of the cold north winds, of which in our exposed position we got the full benefit. There was nothing left to do but dig a hole in the ground. As it would have to be roofed over with our gum blankets, we could only dig it as long and as wide as *they* would permit, and in that hole four of us had to harbor for the winter. We dug it about three feet deep, but could not make it long enough to allow us to straighten out our legs, or wide enough to permit us to lie in any other way than spoon fashion. Our shoulders and hip bones made holes in the ground into which they accurately fitted, and so closely were we packed together that when one turned we all had to turn. Lying all night in our cramped position with no covering, keeping life in each other by our joint contribution of animal heat only, we would come out of the hole in the morning un-

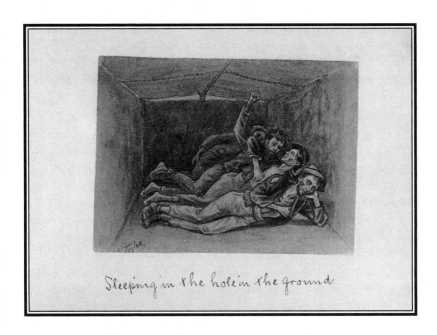

Sleeping in the hole in the ground

able to straighten up until the sun would come out to thaw us and limber our poor sore, stiff joints.

Brennan and I, as the owners of the blankets, were given the inside which had its advantages in one way, and its disadvantages in another. Rapp lay on the outside, next the dirt; Brennan next to him, I next to Brennan, and Beavers on the outside. I was thus sandwiched between Brennan and Beavers. If we could have lain still, we might have kept warmer, but just as soon as we began to sleep a little and be comfortable, the lice would begin to nip us so badly that we were obliged to scratch and dig; this would disturb us and disturb our neighbors. Being between two I had to submit to scratching on both sides of me. Beavers wasn't so bad but Brennan was a terror. Sleeping or awake, it was all the same with him; from head to foot his upper hand would have full range and it was constantly at work. If feeling for his head, he would bump my nose, and in digging around his waistband, he would jab his sharp elbows into my ribs, and in that way, most of the time unconscious of it, he would keep it up all night.

Reproaches, persuasion, and profanity from Rapp and myself were all resorted to, but all were alike failures, and we were obliged to grin and bear it.

We never drew cooked rations in Florence. Everything was uncooked, but as in Andersonville, there was too scanty a ration of wood to cook what we had. We had a pan made from the tin roofing of an old freight car that Nelse Eveland managed to secure on our way from Charleston to Florence, and by clubbing our rations of wood and rations of meal or beans together we were able to get along after a fashion. As soon as we were through, we would loan our pan to someone else, and so that pan would be kept hot nearly all the time.

Having nothing in which to put the mush when it was cooked we were obliged to eat it out of the pan, and in order that we should get no advantage one of the other, we adopted a code of table rules. When the mush was cooked, and the pan taken off the fire, we would seat ourselves around it on the ground and wait for the mush to cool. Boiled mush is a rightly hot dish and holds the heat a long time. It was hard work for us to wait, and long before it was cool enough we would be scraping the flakes off the sides of the pan, impatient to begin. At a given signal each man dipped his spoon into the mush, filled it, and all raised our spoons together. Now came the interesting time; we were very hungry but the mush was so hot we had to take our time—all except Brennan. That fellow had a cast iron mouth. He would take a tablespoonful of scalding hot mush in his mouth, swallow it, and reach for the dish again before we were half through with ours. Often Rapp on one side and I on the other with our mouths full of hot mush and the tears streaming down our cheeks, unable to speak a word, have grabbed Brennan's hands and by signs and force kept his spoon out of the dish until we could get even with him. I have often scalded myself so badly that the skin would hang in shreds from the roof of my mouth.

We had only one meal a day, and as the weather grew colder, we would hold our rations until nearly dark before we cooked them, and then eating our breakfast, dinner, and supper, as hot as we could bear it, would lie down at once and endeavor to get to sleep while the warmth of the food was in us. All through the winter this continued, and this winter was noted as the coldest in that section for many years.

We had no blankets or other covering, and when we were ready to retire for the night, we would take off our blouses and lay them over us, they kept us warmer in that way. Poor old Beavers, however, kicked against taking off his blouse, and we were forced to humor him because he had no shirt. The hole, as I have said, was just wide enough for us to lie in spoon fashion. We all had to lie the same way with the hand under our heads for a pillow, and the upper hand free for defensive purposes, against the common enemy.

After a while our bodies would get so sore and tired that we would be obliged to turn over, and from someone would come the order "spoon right" or "spoon left" and we would all change front to the rear. We got so accustomed to this that we would change frequently while asleep or not thoroughly awake. We four persons lived to get home, and it was only through our sticking by each other and caring for each other that we did so. During the winter, I have frequently, in the early morning when on my way down to the creek to wash, seen

Eating Mush

poor fellows dead along the road or street, frozen to death during the night. They had no comrades to lie with, no place to lie in, and no one to look after them. It did not require extremely cold weather to freeze to death, men in our enfeebled and starving condition.

We suffered most during the cold rains, for our clothing would get soaked with the ice cold water, and we had no wood to build fires except to cook our rations; and frequently we have lain down to sleep in our dugout, only to be awakened during the night with the rain pouring in on us and we lying half body deep in water. You cannot understand the suffering and terrible misery of this period by any description I can give you. It was this: To those of us who lived it was all the torture that hunger, cold, and exposure could give us, short of actual death; but it was even that to hundreds of others who laid down their lives in that earthly hell.

I mean just what I say by the term "laid down their lives," for it was actually and voluntarily so. Often in those bitter cold mornings after a night of indescribable misery, the rebel recruiting agents would come in and offer to any who would go out and take service in the Confederate army, warm clothing, plenty to eat, and comfortable quarters. Here was an opportunity to exchange our miserable lot for what was to us the supremest blessing our hearts could hope for. Is it to be wondered at, and can you condemn men who, weakened under this strain and who in the hopes of saving their lives went out and took the oath of allegiance to the Confederacy? You can take pride, then, in the fact that outside of a few "Raiders" who were despised by prisoners and rebels alike, that the temptations and allurements of the Confederate agents failed to seduce them from their allegiance and duty to their country and their flag; and one of the brightest pages of the history of our Civil War is *that*, where those brave men chose rather to endure the pangs of hunger and cold and disease until death would relieve their sufferings than to swerve from their duty to their flag.

One of the most potent arguments used by these agents was that our government knew of our condition and had refused to exchange us. We did not know of the truth of this, but we did know that if true, there must be some reason for it. It was true in this far. General Grant realized the importance of ending the war at the earliest possible time. He was informed that the Confederacy had all its reserves in the field. He knew that we were being tortured and starved to death. There were 60,000 of us in the hands of the rebels, there were an equal number of rebel prisoners in prisons of the North. We would, if exchanged, have gone to fill the hospitals and homes of the North, but none would have gone to fill the wasted ranks of the armies in the field. They, the rebel prisoners, well fed, well cared for, in as good condition as when they were captured, would have gone to the front at once, the thinned ranks would have been filled up, and the war would have been prolonged indefinitely. General Grant refused to make the exchange. Of course, it was cruel to us, but war is full of cruelties and we were the sacrifice offered to save the boys at the front and to end the war. It was a military necessity and although it meant a miserable death for many of us, we bowed to the inevitable, and remained true to the old flag. You can decide for yourselves what was the value of our services and sacrifices.[5]

Despairing of getting Americans to take service with them, they next turned their attention to the foreigners and undertook to raise a foreign legion. They were not much more successful, although they got some. I will, however, do them justice to say that I do not believe one in a hundred went out except with the intention of taking the first opportunity of escaping and going through to our lines. I know of many who did so. The experience of the rebels with their new recruits was not satisfactory. They deserted at every opportunity, frequently taking the old rebel soldiers along with them until at last, General [William J.] Hardee, disgusted with them, ordered that they should all be returned to the prison. They were known to us and also to the rebels by the name of "Galvanized Yanks" and when word came that they were to be returned to prison, a feeling of resentment against them spread through the prison and it was resolved that they should not have a warm reception.[6] As they were turned into prison and scattered through it, they were set upon and hammered and driven from one place to another until dark came on. In the morning it was almost impossible to tell who were "Galvanized" and who were not, for during the night a general exchange of garments had taken place, and rebel jackets adorned the backs of as many who had not been out as of those who had.

During the time that the rebel agents were endeavoring to secure enlistments, one approached Beavers and talked to the old man and held up to him the glittering prospect of clothing, food, and every other blessing he might desire if he would take the oath of allegiance to the Confederacy. Barefooted, on the frozen ground, without a hat or shirt, having had nothing to eat for twenty-four hours, the old man turned on him at last, and with his eyes blazing in his indignation, he gave that rebel to understand in good vigorous English with a smart sprinkling of undiluted Pennsylvania profanity that if he had him up in Luzerne County, Pennsylvania, for about fifteen minutes, he would permanently retire him from the business of trying to make traitors out of poor, helpless, starving prisoners.

About this time I received an offer to go outside the prison to play the violin for the entertainment of the rebel officers, but I declined the offer as I was determined to stay by the other boys as long as we were in. I knew of another violin player whom I recommended and

Beavers and the rebel recruiting officer

he was taken out. It was an opportunity that was not often rejected, that of getting outside either as one of the wood squad, baker, clerk, butcher, or other occupation. It meant comfortable quarters, more rations, and opportunities for escape. The wood squad cut wood in the swamps for the use of the camp, and as there were no teams [of draft animals], they had to carry it to a point near the gate and pile it up to be distributed later in the day. These men were, many of them, Western men, and good choppers. Outside they had many opportunities of getting beans from the negroes and even from the rebels themselves, and smuggling them inside. They had to smuggle them, for it was forbidden for the prisoners to trade for any articles on sale by the rebel sutler and the penalty was severe whenever discovered.

There were plenty of beans to be had outside at one-third the price charged by the sutler and of course the inducement to trade was strong. At first, beans were carried in haversacks, in pockets, in shirts, and in every receptacle that could be thought of, but all had to be abandoned as the rebels would get on to them. These failing, the boys got to bringing them in in hollow logs. I will explain that each member of the wood squad was allowed to carry a log of wood into camp with him each evening. The rebels wondered for some time why the men insisted on picking out unsound logs instead of sound ones to take into the camp. The mystery was revealed one day when one of the boys lost control of his log, dropped it, the plug came out, and about half a bushel of beans rattled out on the ground. That game was up, and the bean market at the sutler's stand took an upward tendency.

"Necessity was the mother of invention" there as everywhere else, however, and beans were about the biggest necessity we knew of. The hollow log business stopped at once; *that was played out.* None but sound logs were taken into camp afterwards. Before allowing the wood squad to enter camp at the close of the day's work, they were required to form into line, throw down their logs, and submit to a rigid inspection of person and log. For a few days after the hollow log discovery, no beans were taken in, but before long the sutler complained that the boys were not buying so many beans and the guards were urged to greater vigilance. It was explained away by the claim

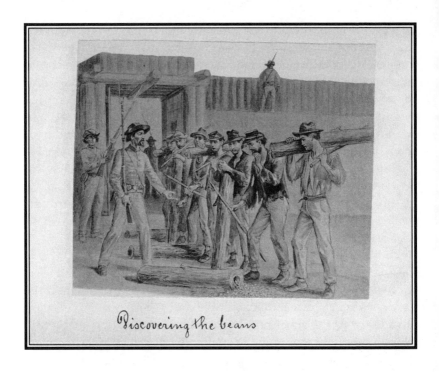

Discovering the beans

that money was getting to be very scarce with the boys; and this explanation for the want of a better one was finally accepted.

The boys had discovered another way, however. As anxious as we were to get beans, quite a number of the rebel soldiers were anxious to sell them to us and they found abundant opportunities to open up trade with the boys, and make it easy to get the beans into camp. It occurred to one of the boys that it would be possible to split an ash or pine log through the center and hollow out both sides into a trough if there was any way to fasten the halves together again, for nails or gimlets we had none. He found a rebel who had beans to sell and broached the idea to him. After thinking a little while, the rebel recollected a little graveyard or other enclosure not far away with a picket fence around it, and thought perhaps some nails could be got out of them. He went away and returned in a little while with a few rusty nails, which, although not very good, would answer the purpose. The "yank" and the "reb" went to work together and in a short time had split and hollowed the log. Splitting a three cornered plug out of one end and then joining it together so as to have the bark cover the signs of the split, they turned it upon end and poured the beans from the bag into the log. The log held more than the bag and the space must be filled with something or the beans might rattle loud enough to attract attention. Stuffing in moss and grass to fill it as far as they could, they drove the plug in, dabbed that end in the mud, and to all appearances it was as honest a log as ever went into prison. Mr. Yank shouldered it at the proper time and reported at the gate with the rest of the squad.

As ill luck would have it, the meanest rebel Lieutenant of the prison, Lt. Barrett, inspected the squad that evening and something prompted him to take particular notice of this log.[7] He stood on it and it turned with him, nearly throwing him, and rolled about ten feet away. Josiah Wolfe, the owner of the log, expecting it couldn't stand the strain, moved away, intending to disown it; the log, however, stuck together and after a few wicked oaths leveled at the log and the man that cut it, Barrett moved on to torment someone else.[8] Josiah shouldered his log and marched into prison that night, one of the proudest men in camp. This occurred a little while after I got outside on parole and Bill Mills, a comrade of mine in the wood squad, got word to me that I must get him some nails.[9]

There was a car shop along the railroad between the prison and Florence town in which an old colored man was building a freight car, and I thought I could, maybe, pick up a few nails there on the floor. I strolled down there at the first opportunity and fortunately found the old man at work, but not a nail could I find on the floor. I finally told the old man I wanted a few nails. He said they were very scarce, all he had was in a "kaig on the other side of the cyah and he dah not give one away, and the gahdes were so strick about taking any that if he saw me take any he would have to report me to de camp." He immediately turned his back and walked to the other end of the shed and my hand went into the keg and came out full again in a hurry. Stowing them in my shirt and bidding the old man goodbye, I got up to camp just in time to slip them into Bill Mills' blouse as he was shouldering his log. It was a long time before the rebels succeeded in catching on to this game, but they finally found it out.

It was then forbidden to take any whole logs in, but it was only a day or two before the boys found it was just as easy to split a thin slab off the front of a split log, dig out a trough, fill the cavity with beans, lay the slab back carefully, and fasten it on with a few nails, and with the exception that it did not hold as much as a whole log, it answered the purpose just as well. This plan lasted until a few days before the prison was abandoned.

In Florence as in Andersonville, many tunnels were started, but very few prisoners ever escaped by them. There were quite a number dug in the thousand to which I belonged, but bad luck attended all of them as far as I ever knew. They would be started in some tent and the work would be done by night and the dirt taken out would be carried down and emptied in the creek. The rebels were constantly on the search for tunnels, and it was necessary to try every dodge to throw them off the track. Generally a sick man, or a blanket in the daytime, would be placed over the mouth of the tunnel, and all traces of the night's work would be obliterated. Suspecting that a tunnel was being dug, and not being able to locate it, Lt. Barrett gave orders that no rations should be issued to our thousand until we revealed the tunnel and gave up the offenders to him for punishment. He was correct enough in his *suspicions,* tunnels were being dug, but the boys were loyal to each other and no information came to Barrett. Those who knew would not tell, and those who didn't know looked wise and said nothing.

We were getting at this time only about a pint of coarse ground corn meal a day, and for over a hundred days in Florence there was scarcely any variation from this issue. We were rotting with scurvy for want of change of food, and starving day by day for the want of the food itself, miserable as it was. Many could not control themselves sufficiently to wait after receiving their rations until they could cook them, but would eat their corn meal raw. It did them, of course, but little good, and when they got in that condition they soon died. I noticed in particular, one man, who, on drawing his corn meal, would sit down on the ground and eat it like a famished wolf, and when it was gone, would cry like a child. All manhood was gone. He knew nothing now but the intense gnawing day and night that could not be satisfied. I learned his name was Staples, and he was from someplace near Stroudsburg, Pa. He died soon after.

This was our condition when by the inhuman order of Lt. Barrett, our issue of rations were stopped. One day passed and night came on, and we lay down in vain hopes that sleep might come to us, but our hunger was too intense. We would drink water until we could drink no more, in the endeavor to obtain relief. After a while I did drop off, but for only a little time, and during that time I dreamed of home and of eating, eating without any satisfaction, and then I awoke to face the miserable reality. To increase our suffering, it came on to rain on the second day, and wet and cold, no food, no fire, scantily clad, we stood around and suffered; oh, God only knows how we suffered. We were weak and our limbs would tremble under us as we tried to walk about. We could look at each other, but we could not talk to each other, we had got beyond that; we were suffering too intensely. We came on to the third day. The rain had done its work and had revealed a tunnel by caving it in. In the afternoon late, rations were issued to us again, and 76 hours from the time we had eaten before, we surrounded our little pan to eat our scanty ration of mush. It was only the regular ration, nothing extra for what we had lost. A ration lost for any cause was lost forever in Florence. Those three days sent many a poor fellow to his grave, and of all the suffering I endured during my prison life, nothing equaled it.

Before the war I was acquainted with an engineer on the D.L.&W. R.R. [Delaware Lackawanna, and Western Railroad] by the name of Andrew Jackson. When the war broke out, he enlisted in the 50th Penna. Vols., and was captured, I think, in Virginia.[10] To my great relief, I met him one day in Florence, and he invited me to come to his tent sometime and have a talk with him. Being in his neighborhood the day after our long fast, I paid my visit. He drew from me what had been undergoing in our thousand, and offered me his sympathy, which seemed to be all he had. He said he was not feeling well, and asked me if I would not read an old *Harpers* magazine to him awhile, while he mixed himself a little gruel. I was only too glad to do it. He was a sergeant of a hundred and had saved a little wheat flour. Sergeants had double rations. He mixed himself a ration of flour, and commenced to cook it over his little fire. I read to him a part of [Charles] Dickens' "Bleak House" and we both became very much interested as I read. I kept one eye on the gruel all the time, however, and imagined to myself how good that would taste when it was done—to him—not to me, for not a thought that I would have any part of it entered my head. Hungry as I had been, I never in all my prison life asked for anything to eat. We, none of us, ever did that. We all realized that food was one thing no one had to spare.

Andrew was very deliberate in his movements; he even dusted a little salt in and for flavor, a little piece of red pepper, and then to cap it all, put a little piece of bacon, about as big as a half dollar, to give it richness. Here was a mess that was beyond all, the richest I had ever dreamed of, or heard of, or seen while I had been in prison. Wheat flour, could anything under the blue canopy be nicer—and salt—and pepper—and bacon. Andrew was apparently unconscious of my thoughts, and was buried in his cooking. At last, "Bleak House" was ended, and not wishing to sit around watching another man eat, I arose to go. He insisted on my sitting still a little longer while he cooled the gruel. When it was sufficiently cooled, he tasted it thoroughly to satisfy himself that it was properly seasoned and then passed it over to me, saying, "I don't feel very well today and I guess you had better dispose of this for me." I saw through it all. It had been intended for me all the time. I could not thank him by any words, but the tears that blinded my eyes and dropped in the pan told him how I felt. I can never forget Andrew Jackson. Do you wonder? I have met him twice since the war. The first time when I was in the grip of the prison fever after I got home; the other time was two years ago when he came all the way from Missouri to attend the annual banquet of our Union Ex-Prisoners of War Association of Lackawanna County, Pa.

The great scarcity of wood and our great need of it compelled us to make every shift to get it and we would dig down in the swamp for roots until it seemed impossible that any roots could be left. The wood issued to us was maple, ash, gumwood, and pine. The maple and gumwood were almost useless to us, as we had no axes and could not split or cut them up. The pine was the best, as it was full of pitch and burned with a hotter blaze than the other kinds. The effect of burning the pitch pine wood was to blacken our faces and mat our hair with soot until we could not be distinguished in color from the negroes. The water alone would not wash this black smoke off our faces, and as we had no soap, it kept accumulating layer by layer un-

Before and after shaving

til it was pretty well packed on. At one time I did some favor for one of the boys who had a razor and to repay me he offered to give me a shave. Not having experienced such a luxury in six months, and my face being covered with hair, I accepted the invitation. The effect was unexpected and striking. Where the razor had traversed my face it had taken off the beard and left the skin clean and white. The rest of my face was in "darkest Africa," and you can imagine how I must have looked.

When I was captured I had an excellent pair of boots for which I refused many tempting offers, and knowing that if we remained in prison during the winter I would need them much more than during the summer, I saved them up against the time of need and went barefooted. In the meantime the scurvy had fastened its grip on me and my feet and legs had become very much swollen, so that when the winter set in I was unable to get my feet in the boots and I was obliged to part with them. All the old prisoners had the scurvy bad by this time and their condition was miserable in the extreme. Our teeth were loose and the gums receding from the teeth. Ugly sores were breaking out on us and our flesh was so lifeless that every pressure of the flesh on our swollen limbs would leave an indentation the same as if made in a roll of butter, or other inelastic substance, and it would be a considerable time before the indentation would remove.

I was now hatless and shoeless and my shirt-sleeves had been cut off to mend the body of my shirt; my pantaloons, which were tight around the waist when I was captured, I now clasped around and buttoned on the side button after buckling them up as tight as I could. About this time a lot of goods sent through our lines by the Christian Sanitary Commission were received at Florence, and we were notified that they would be distributed among us.[11] We were among the

A case of scurvy

first called out. The clothing consisted of woolen shirts, drawers, socks, and Burnside hats. There were not enough to give each one a full outfit, and therefore they would get only that which was most needed, or if they seemed tolerably well provided for, would not get anything. I hid my blouse in a hole in our dugout. It was a cold, frosty morning, and the sun had not made his presence felt much as yet. As we stood in line we looked miserable enough, but not to compare with the way we felt. We had not got straightened out yet after the night, as we stood in line each bent like a letter "S" our poor, lean, skinny arms clasped around us to keep our bodies from shaking apart, teeth chattering and knees knocking together, we were anything but happy.

Our rebel sergeant was a real good, kind-hearted fellow and he was as sorry for us as he could be, and I know favored us as far as he could. When he came to me, he said, "Well, what do you want most?" I chattered out "Everything." I had no hat, my shirt was sleeveless and the body as thin as a sheet of paper, patched and full of holes, my pantaloons were in about the same condition, and the bottoms were tied around my ankles with pieces of rope; I had no drawers and I was barefooted. "Well," he said, "the best thing I can give you is a shirt," and he handed me a long grey woolen shirt that was almost as long as a nightshirt. Among other things that helped to keep me alive that winter, there was nothing to which I owe more than to that blessed old long, grey warm woolen shirt.

I did not see Rapp, Brennan, or Beavers until I got back to the dugout. I thought, of course, that each would have something, and especially Beavers, who had no shirt at all, but when we came together to compare notes I found they had neither of them drawn a single thing and they felt dreadfully about it, as they had good cause. The woman who made that shirt I drew had no idea, and probably never has had any knowledge, of the great amount of comfort it afforded one poor, hungry, shivering mortal. If she only knew the half of it, she would have felt amply repaid.

In a few days we were notified that further distribution of sanitary goods would be made, as they had not been entirely exhausted in the first distribution. When our day came I was prepared for it. I buried the new shirt and my blouse in the floor of the dugout, and

Drawing the Sanitary Commission Shirt

equipped the same as before, passed examination again. Directly after our other issue, the rebel sergeant who had distributed the goods to our 1,000 was sent away and we had another sergeant this time. My luck held good again, and this time I drew a red flannel shirt. I think each of the boys (our mess) drew something this time, except Beavers—he was again unlucky. When we came back to our quarters the poor old man felt very sick. He was downhearted and hopeless for the first time during our imprisonment, and I knew it would not do to let him remain that way long, or he could not live. As we were getting ready to lie down that night I told Beavers to put on the shirt and try how it fitted. He didn't wait for a second invitation, for the night was cold, and he needed it badly enough. So attached had Beavers got to that shirt by the next morning that I didn't have the heart to separate them. I believe he would have died had it not been for it.

There was one thing that seemed to puzzle the rebels a great deal and which was truly to one uninitiated, a great mystery. In spite of the deaths in the prison of from 20 to 40 each day, the numbers did not seem to decrease any. The roll of one morning would show, say, 10,000 prisoners in the stockade. Thirty would be taken out dead during the day; no new prisoners would come in, yet the roll call of the next morning would show there were still 10,000 in the prison; and so it would continue to the mystification of the officers and the great discomfort of the rebel sergeants. To ascertain the actual number of prisoners present, a general counting-off would be ordered which would consume nearly an entire day, and which would reveal the fact that the rebels had been issuing several hundred more daily rations than there were prisoners. The trouble would only be remedied for a day or two when there would be another botheration in the count with no chance to detect where the trouble lay. To those who knew, there was nothing strange about it, but they were not inclined to tell.

Each rebel sergeant had a thousand to call roll for and count each morning. The thousands were subdivided into hundreds and he would begin with the first hundred. As soon as that hundred were counted they would break ranks, and he would go on to the next hundred and so on through his thousand. A man could answer roll call and be counted in the first hundred of the first thousand and slip around and answer and be counted in the third or fourth hundred of the fourth thousand, and even again in the eighth thousand without the rebel sergeant being any the wiser. This was called flanking and lots of the boys were engaged in it. The temporary cure for it, and only temporary, would be a general counting off which was done in this way. The prison was divided nearly in the center by a stream, and through the prison at right angles with the stream ran a causeway and a bridge. There was no other way of getting across the bog and the stream. When the rebels wanted to have a general count, they would come in and drive us all over on one side of the prison until we were all counted. This would, of course, if done accurately, give an exact count of all present and would prevent flanking for a few days, until a number of the prisoners had died, when the flankers would begin to appear in the various hundreds answering to the dead men's names, and then before long the last state would be as bad as the first.

When the day of the Presidential Election in November, 1864, came around, we were told by the rebs that we would be given an opportunity of voting for the man of our choice just so as to see how the camp stood. We were always very distrustful of anything the rebs would propose to us, we felt they would not be fair, and that every proposition they might make no matter how fair it might appear on the surface had a sting concealed about it somewhere. We therefore waited patiently and watched. It was as we suspected. At the hour set for the election, a bag of white and a bag of black beans were brought in, 2nd, we were given to understand that those who wanted to vote for McClellan should vote in a white bean, those for Lincoln a black bean. The raiders, the bounty jumpers, and toughs who had managed to hold together a sort of organization by holding in with the rebs were promptly on the ground shouting for McClellan, and ready to intimidate those who wanted to vote for "OLD ABE."

Word was sent through the prison for every man who loved his government and hated the rebs to come out and vote for Lincoln. This

Counting off the Camp

vote was to be sent through the country to show that we denounced the policy of our Government, and considered the war a failure if McClellan had a majority. In a short time the polls were surrounded by a local band of boys that neither reb guards nor N.Y. toughs could intimidate, and every man who came to the polls was made to understand the situation. It was a disheartening defeat to the Johnnies. There were thousands of black beans and only a few hundred white ones. There were those who voted for Lincoln there who would have voted for McClellan perhaps at home, but they were not disposed to give any aid and comfort to the enemy in that way. As evidence that this was a scheme carefully studied beforehand was the fact that the same thing was tried in every prison in the Confederacy—and the result was the same wherever it was tried. The returns were never published by the rebs.

Chapter Five

One day a friend of mine came for me to go on the other side of the creek to try a violin which was there. I did not require much urging, I assure you, for I had not had hold of one since leaving Andersonville, and I felt as if I would enjoy playing a little. I found when I got over there a violin perfect in shape and workmanship (except that the wood had not been varnished) and it was a very fair tone. It was owned by a Canadian Irishman by the name of Duffy, and had been bought by him of a German violin maker who had made it in prison with no other tools than an inch gauge and a jack knife. I played on it with great comfort to myself and with many evidences of pleasure by Duffy and his friends. It secured me a piece of corn pone and an invitation to come again the next day.

Punctually the next day I was on hand and secured another supplement to my rations and another invitation for another day. I was in luck, and if ever a fellow meant to nurse a good job, I meant to nurse this one. It often happens, however, when a man strikes a good thing, there is someone ready to come in and by competition knock his business concave. When I came over on the third day, I found another artist had jumped my claim, and I was out of a job. I felt very sorry for this, for it was literally taking the bread out of my mouth. The new fiddler didn't aim to play anything but jigs, but he played these with a vigor and a dash that completely knocked my playing in the shade. He was a young Irishman and he could play Irish jigs as well as ever I heard them played and I knew enough to know that I had no chance against him. I made the best of my disappointment

Presidential election Novr. 1864

and did the best I could when it came my turn to play. There were those who liked my playing the best, but they had no corn bread to offer.

A few days later I was invited over one evening to the other side of the prison to a hut where some of the 1st Rhode Island Artillery stayed, and there I found the jolliest crowd of fellows I ever met in prison. Here was also a counterpart of Duffy's violin, made by the same man. The strings and bows had been bought in Charleston by a rebel sergeant and had cost the modest sum of $80.00. This violin belonged to a person to whom I will refer to later. We had music, vocal and instrumental, recitations, and speeches. It was a very pleasant evening spent there, and I found some very pleasant and profitable acquaintances, as it turned out. One was Collins Thompson, through whose instrumentality I got out on parole a couple months later, and another was the owner of the violin.[12] His name, I have forgotten, for which I am very sorry, but really that makes very little difference, as it was an assumed one. He noticed the swollen condition of my feet, and that I had no shoes or socks. Before leaving that night he invited me to come to his hut next morning. His hut or tent was just at the gate, the first one inside from the deadline, on the right, coming in. It was probably one of the best huts in the prison. I was much surprised when he produced a pair of slippers and made me a present of them. He said he had tried to get me a pair of shoes, but could not find a pair in prison, and the slippers were the best he could get. I was very thankful indeed, and felt that I could not do enough to show it. It turned out that he was from Reading, Pa., was well acquainted with the family of my comrade John Rapp, but Rapp did not know him, and he would not reveal himself to Rapp.

I soon came to know this much of his history. He was a bounty jumper, had made a great deal of money even in prison, and, I afterwards learned, took away with him about $7,000 in Greenbacks. He was well known in a business way by the rebels outside, and could get anything he wanted of them. He was of a generous, reckless nature, and sudden and fervent in his likes and dislikes. He had bought a great many pair of shoes for the poor fellows in prison, during the winter, and had done many other acts of kindness. He had two comrades; one was a French Canadian going by the name of Jack Girard, a bounty jumper also, a good-hearted, clever fellow, very much attached to his friends and entirely under his influence and control.[13] He was a good cook, very quiet in his way, but always very attentive to what was going on around him. The Boss, as I am obliged to call him, formed a great liking for Rapp and me, and told us to come and see him as often as we pleased. This was not an invitation to be slighted, and we did not intend to slight it. *Business* called us over there quite often. These men, being wealthy, could afford three meals a day.

One day, I got there just a little before their dinner hour, and the Boss asked me to come in and play a few tunes on the violin for them. I was glad enough to do this, and I enjoyed it as much as they seemed to. When the dinner was ready, they gave me a dish of bean soup that had about two ordinary days rations in it—and such bean soup. I don't believe that the best meal that ever tickled the palate of the greatest epicure that ever lived could compare with the taste of this bean soup. My mouth even now waters at the very recollection of it.

Where was Duffy's corn bread alongside of this now? Of course as large as the meal was, it only filled a corner of the long-disused apartments of my stomach, and if I could have had more, I would have kept Jack cooking all the afternoon; but it was fortunate for me that I could not have all I wanted, or I would have killed myself. The other comrade of my friend was Bill Mills of the 1st Wisconsin, of whom I have spoken in connection with the bean log speculation. This was my first meeting with him.

About this time we began to hear rumors of exchange, at first indefinite and vague but gathering strength and shape each day until it was authoritatively announced that there was to be a special exchange of 10,000 of those most broken down and sick. An appeal to the rebel sergeant confirmed this report, and we were told it was going to commence soon. Rapp and I went to consult our friend the Boss about the situation, and he assured us it was true, and that he and Jack were going to try and get away with the rest. I could not see that they were very much broken down, or very sick, but from what I knew of them, I thought they knew what they were talking about.

Bill Mills came over while we were talking, and the Boss said to Bill, "Now, if we any of us get away, we must let these boys come in here and we will leave them what we have to live on." It was agreed then and there that this should be the case, and it made us very happy to know that we were to have such good fortune, although we hoped to get off in the exchange ourselves. At last, one day in the latter part of November, the order came, and we went out to be examined for exchange. We were drawn up in two ranks, and the rebel sergeants went down the lines, carefully noting the condition of each one and questioning such as they selected, as to whether their time was out or not, what state they were from, canvassing the chances of their going into service again, and being careful to exclude such as appeared to be healthy and vigorous and likely to go into the army again in a short time.

While we were being examined, the surgeons in the hospital were selecting there such as could endure the fatigue of the ride to Charleston. We four, Brennan, Beavers, Rapp, and I stood together, and as the Surgeon approached us, I have no doubt they were doing what I was doing myself, fervently praying that I might be chosen. Beavers was examined and rejected. Brennan looked too tough also and was passed. My heart sank down as my turn came and turned to leave as the Surgeon passed me also. Something in Rapp's appearance attracted the attention of the Surgeon. He halted and ordered Rapp to step forward. "How long have you been in the army?" "Three years, sir." "How long have you to serve?" "My time was out two months ago." "Will you re-enlist?" "No, I have got the scurvy all through me; it will take me a year at least, to get well." "How old are you?" "Twenty years." "Where do you live?" "Pennsylvania." "Well, I reckon you can go."

We were rejoiced for Rapp's sake, but sorry to have him leave us. We bade him good-bye, and with heavy hearts turned our faces to the stockade. I have never seen Rapp since. I hope to sometime if the Lord wills. He was a good, true friend and a brave soldier.

We understood that there would be other drafts, so that outside of a little temporary depression from which we tried to rally each other, we suffered no ill effects. The effect on many of the poor, suf-

Parole of John Rapp

fering fellows was the very worst, however, in many cases. There were a great many deaths as the result of this disappointment. As soon as we got settled down, I went over to see what luck the Boss had. I found Bill Mills there, feeling very blue, as he had also been rejected. The Boss and Jack Girard had been taken to act as nurses for the sick. Bill told me that a silver watch given to one of the rebel sergeants or surgeons did the business for them, and got them through. Bill and I had fallen heir to a grand estate, and we entered at once on our inheritance. It consisted of a tent made of two woolen blankets and with another blanket inside to put over us, and a pan; and better than all, about a peck of beans. This was great wealth in prison.

Bill did not exactly relish my coming in as an equal partner, however, and I, recognizing his prior claims, did not insist on my rights, but thought if I got the privilege of staying in the comfortable shelter alone it would be a great gain for me, and we would get along pleasantly together, and he came to like me and I him, very much; and the old love was that strong that he came, several years ago, to the national encampment at Milwaukee, from Minneapolis, on purpose to meet me there and talk over our old trials and experiences. When we met, our eyes filled with tears and our voices choked up so that we could not speak a word. We could only clasp each other's hands and by dumb show give evidence of our joy at meeting again. After a while, however, our tongues were loosened and questions came thick and fast concerning old comrades and the scenes and incidents of the old life, until we were too tired to talk more. . . .

Brennan and Beavers now had the old dugout all to themselves, and having more room, could scratch to their heart's content, but they suffered more from the cold now that Rapp and I were out. In a few days another examination took place, and this time they were both taken and I was the only one left. I was now almost alone in the stockade. My early comrades were all gone or dead, and I began to be despondent at times. Bill was in the wood squad and drew double rations, but he had a hearty appetite and could eat all he drew without any trouble. All I had, more than I had before, was better shelter. This, of course, was a great help, but it did not help hunger. The sickness, insanity, and deaths in the prison now were frightful, far exceeding the worst period of Andersonville while we were there.

Fever and Insanity

The great mental strain and the extreme disappointment, together with the terrible suffering from hunger and exposure, was too much for many and the prison fever soon had many in its clutches. Few recovered from it. In the delirium of the fever, men would run wildly and blindly across the prison until utterly exhausted, they would fall down and die where they had fallen. Frequently, two or three would be found lying dead together in some hut or dugout.

Ordinarily, death did not come hard. Men would pass away easily and peacefully; they simply ran until the machinery refused to run any longer, and they quit living. Except when they had the fever, their minds would be tolerably clear up to death. When not disturbed, their thoughts would turn to home, and their last words were loving messages to the dear ones they were never more to meet or see on earth. With very many, reason gave away, and men wandered around aimlessly and vacantly, knowing nor noticing nothing that was passing around them, fancying they were at home or somewhere else than in prison. Such a condition would only be for a short time, however. Death would soon claim them and they would go to join the vast army of martyrs.

Short of death, the thing we most dreaded was gangrene. Any abrasion of the skin of the feet or legs would be apt to bring this on. We had no medicines or remedies of any kind in the prison proper, and very little more in the hospital. When a sore gangrened, it became very painful. A distinct line separating the sound from the diseased flesh would show itself, the latter being, in some cases, as black as ebony. After a while the diseased flesh would slough away from the other. The bones would protrude white and glistening. Toes and feet would drop off, and the poor victims would be helpless. Many thus afflicted died there. A few lived to get through to our lines to give indisputable evidence of their terrible condition, while one notable case is living yet. John January lost both feet by gangrene and came through to our lines a veritable bag of bones.[14] By good nursing he recovered, and is now a big, hearty man minus both feet. He is living somewhere in the West.

Gangrene cases

The third and last examination for exchange drew near. We all knew that in this would lie our last hopes of exchange before the end of the war, and we were correspondingly anxious to get out. I had thought of this so much that I had about made up my mind that I must be successful this time, or I would have to give up the fight for existence further. I had talked it over with a comrade named Fairchild of Kingston, Pa. (he was known by us all by the name of Pusher), and he felt much as I did. Pusher had been remarkably cheerful and lighthearted under the most trying circumstances all through his imprisonment and often declared his determination to live it out and spite the rebels. He had parted with all his comrades as I had, some by death, and a number in the previous exchanges until he felt that he must get away. He could not stand it. We were in about the same physical condition. I may have had a little more strength than he had, but not a great deal. We talked over what we would do when we got home again, and how we would enjoy our Christmas dinner among our friends, and how we would enjoy ourselves once more, and planned a great many things for the future.

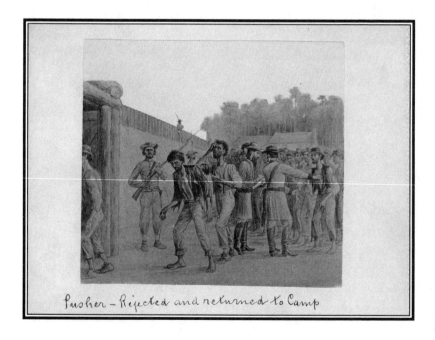

Pusher – Rejected and returned to Camp

The next day we went out together for our last chance, and to our great sorrow and dismay we were rejected and turned back into the prison. I cannot describe our feelings. It was as if we had been given a glimpse of heaven only to be cast down to hell. We had built so much on our getting home, and we were so tired and sick of the eternal hunger and suffering. We were both hopeless and heartbroken and not we alone, but many more were just like us. We separated as we got inside the prison, and went to our respective places too sad to say anything to each other. It was some time before I could rally enough to think of anything but my extreme misery, but at last something within me seemed to say, "Be a man; don't let the rebs have the satisfaction of burying you like a dog. Brace up and spite them by living." I reasoned with myself that if I continued in this state the end would come soon, and by exercising all the will power I had, got myself upon my feet and out in the night air, and commenced to walk around the camp. I found some of my acquaintances and we consoled each other and strengthened each other with resolves to live while we could see anybody else live.

In the morning I went to the place where the dead were gathered before being taken out of the stockade, to see if any of my friends were among them. What a long line there was of them this morning. It was more than double the number, and there, almost among the first I came to, was poor Pusher. His disappointment was too great, and he could not bear up under it. When a man lost hope, his days were numbered. The *determination* to live kept many brave souls up and carried them through the fight.

In the same line with us on the last day of exchange was a tall Kentuckian whose name I have forgotten. He belonged to the 1st Kentucky Cavalry, and like all the loyal Kentuckians and Tennesseeans he was intensely loyal, indeed. Between the rebel and Union border-state men there existed the bitterest hatred, and it flashed out wherever there was the least occasion. This man had been a prisoner a long time. He was worn down by starvation and bent and cramped by disease. He was scurvied from head to foot, and but for his indomitable spirit would have been dead long before. He said he didn't come there to die, and he'd be dog-goned if he would die. As the Surgeon came to him, he told him to step to the front. He inquired

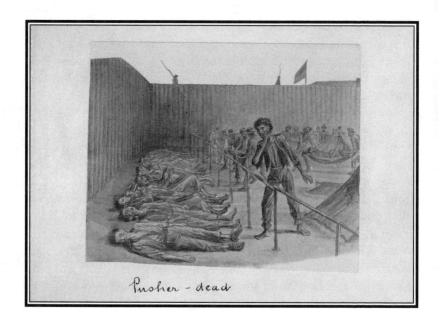

Pusher - dead

how long he had been a prisoner. He answered about a year and a half. "How long have you got to serve yet?" "My time has been out more than six months." "Will you go into service again?" "Well, no, not likely." "Well, I reckon you can go." "What regiment do you belong to?" "The First Kentucky Cavalry." "What! The First Kentucky Cavalry—step back there. We will keep you d——d Kentuckians and Tennesseeans to the last." Kentuck stepped back into line, and straightening himself up as well as his stiffened joints and cords would allow, turned on the rebel Surgeon and with concentrated bitterness said, "Johnny, you can keep me and be d——d. I will outlive your d——d Confederacy." The compliments that passed between these gentlemen for a few minutes were highly flavored, and if not elegant were very pointed and forcible. Kentuck kept his word. He did live to outlive the Confederacy, and I hope he is living today. When we were exchanged in March, we brought him through the lines in a blanket, too weak to walk, but just as plucky as ever.

The civil government inside of Florence prison was very good in some respects. We were kept in some kind of order and there was more regard for the cleanliness of the camp than in Andersonville, but the men placed over us as police were in many instances more brutal than the rebels themselves. There was one particularly offensive brute by the name of Stanton. He was of a New York State regiment. His complexion and hair were in color and general style decidedly African, but I do not think there was any negro blood in him. At any rate, I would not like to disgrace the negroes by any such charge or intimation. Stanton seemed to want to please his rebel masters and thought the surest passport to their favor was by beating and abusing his weak and suffering fellow prisoners. He would club a man for no cause, or knock a poor fellow down and then give him a kicking for some insignificant offense. The poor fellows, weak and suffering, dare make no resistance, for he always had a gang of his loafers who would back him up.

When we were exchanged, Stanton dare not come through with us. I do not know where he went, but he turned up in parole camp, Annapolis, a month or so later, one day. As he had not changed

The big Kentuckian and the rebel officer

much, he was easily recognized, and he had not been there long
when a little fellow came up to him and said, "Mr. Stanton, do you
remember me?" Stanton said, "No, I do not, indeed." "Well," he said,
"I will refresh your memory. Do you recollect one day in prison, that
you clubbed a little fellow down by the bridge, and that he told you
there would be a settling day hereafter?" Stanton denied all knowledge of the occurrence. By this time a great crowd of paroled prisoners began to gather around, and among them, many who recognized Stanton, and one fellow sang out, "I was there and saw him do
it." "Well," said the little fellow (his name was Potter and he belonged
to a Pennsylvania regiment), "I will not take the advantage of you that
you did of me, but I am going to thrash you just the same." Stanton
turned as pale with fear as his coppery hide would permit and tried
to get away from his enemy, but it was no use. Potter kept his word
to the letter. He did everlastingly thrash Stanton, and he did his work
clean and handsomely. Stanton could not stay in camp; as soon as it
became known he was there, there were many who had suffered at
his hands who wanted to settle with him as Potter had, and he had
to put himself under the protection of the officers of the camp and
be taken away.

In prison we were cut off from the world and knew but little of
the progress of the war except as we could get it from the prisoners
who were being brought in daily, either from Sherman's army, or
from the scattered posts in the rear. The news as we got it from *rebel*
sources was very discouraging, but whenever we could get close
enough to a *slave* to speak to him we heard a different story. We
learned that Sherman had started on a big raid through Georgia and
the rebels told us big stories of what they were going to do with him.
In a few days some prisoners were brought in who had been captured
at isolated posts in the rear of Sherman, and their stories rather confirmed the rebel statements. They were 100-day men from Ohio and
had not been in the service more than a month when they were captured. Their clothes were new, and good, and clean, and the bright
blue did look good to us, but it was not half as blue as they were when
they came into the stockade and saw what was before them. The
rebels told us about Hood having got in behind Sherman, destroyed
his communications, torn up the railroads, captured the garrisons

in his rear, and that he was chasing Thomas hot foot towards Nashville, and if he caught him before he got there, there would not be a grease spot left of his army. He would then turn back and overtake Sherman and wipe him from the face of the earth, and as that was all England and France were waiting for, they would then immediately recognize the Confederacy, the Confederate ports would be opened, and the war would be virtually over. It was a good plan, an excellent plan, and but for the mulishness of Thomas and Sherman would have succeeded perhaps? Hood *did* catch Thomas at Franklin, and he wasn't satisfied after he caught him, and he even regretted it exceedingly, for it interfered materially with the nice plan which had been laid out, for when he had caught Thomas he couldn't let go so easily, and when Thomas got through with him there was no rebel army left to follow Sherman, and so that very unpopular General and his bummers waltzed along through the sunny South towards the seaboard with no opposition that to them seemed worthy of notice, and the rest of the plan could not be carried out.

Fiddling the wood squad into camp

But we were not getting the daily papers at this time, and we did not know all the particulars. After a while we noticed the rebels had no more news for us and they did not appear happy, and we knew there was good news if we could only get it. We got it from the next prisoners that came in. We learned of the battle of Franklin and of Sherman's march towards the sea, and with all our strength we cheered, and we raised together our cracked and feeble voices in all the patriotic songs we knew. How we could have enjoyed singing "Marching Through Georgia" if we had only known it. It was not in existence yet, but it was well on the way. After this we got no news for a long time.

I was Bill Mills' partner now and looked after the tent while he was in the wood squad during the day. I used to draw and cook our rations and try to have them ready by the time he would come in. I had a fiddle, and while the beans were boiling I would play to pass the time away. Our tent was close to the deadline and the gate. One day I was playing in this way as the wood detail commenced to carry the wood into the camp. Col. Iverson was on top of the embankment at the gate, and told one of the boys to call me out to fiddle for the boys while they were bringing in the wood.[15] It was quite a novel thing to do, but it helped the work along and the boys all seemed to enjoy it too. After the wood had all been carried in, Col. Iverson told me I might have a log for myself as a reward. I was very glad, indeed, to avail myself of this offer. Depositing my fiddle in the tent, I started for the wood pile. I selected the biggest log I could find and undertook to shoulder it, but I found my ambition had exceeded my strength, for I could neither raise it to my shoulder nor stand up under it when I got there. But I was determined to have it, and the wrestle commenced. I foiled with it, sometimes one on top, sometimes the other, and if ever a poor, weak fellow struggled in this world, I did for a time, getting that log into camp. I got there at last and sat down to blow and rest. I felt proud and tired enough to die. Imagine my disappointment when one of the boys came along and said to me, "Partner, you worked mighty hard for your log, but it will not do you much good." "Why?" said I. "Well, because it is a gum wood and it will neither split or cut." If this was true, my work was as good as wasted, for it was true that having neither axe or hatchet it was im-

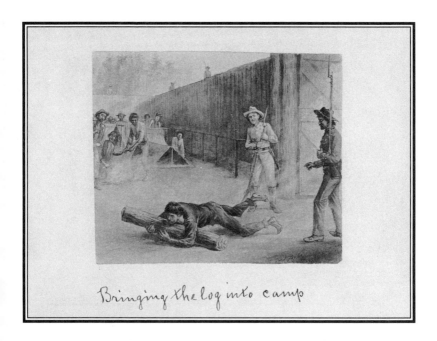

Bringing the log into camp

possible to split a gum log. Bill Mills, however, came in and settled the question very soon. He pronounced it an ash log and soon demonstrated it by splitting it from end to end with a small wedge.

That night a good many of the boys came around, and at their request I played for them, and in a little while they formed sets, and in the blaze of the guard fires two or three hundred of them danced along between the deadline and the huts, as far as the sound of the violin could reach, while hundreds of the boys for a short time forgot their misery and looked on and enjoyed the ball, while the stockade on the outside was crowded with rebel officers and guards looking on and enjoying it as much as anyone else. What a dance that was. The poor fellows limping through the measures, their rags fluttering in the wind and their smoke-begrimed faces and matted hair showing weird and uncanny in the firelight, it was a sight once seen never to be forgotten. It is a pity that some poet cannot immortalize it as did Bobby Burns the witches dance in Tam O'Shanter.[16]

The next day, while engaged in my afternoon's job, boiling the mush, and playing the fiddle to help it along, the corner of the blan-

The dance at the dead-line

ket was lifted, and I was asked to come outside. On coming out and getting to the light I found it was the Adjutant of the camp, Adjutant Cheatham.[17] This officer was generally liked by the prisoners, for he was uniformly kind and good tempered and had a good word for us, if he had nothing else to offer. The Adjutant asked me if I did not want to go outside to play for the entertainment of the officers. I replied that I could not tell until I had talked to my partner about it, and asked him if he could give me until the wood squad would come in to decide. He very pleasantly replied in the affirmative, and promised to come in again at that time.

In the meantime, I set to thinking over the offer, and considering the chances. I was alone. All my old comrades were dead or exchanged. I was filled with scurvy, nearly destitute of clothing, and the cords of my legs had contracted so that I could not stand erect. We all understood that there would be no more exchanges to the end of the war, and I thought that if I ever wanted to see home and friends again, I had better accept the offer. The only question that was in the way was as to whether or not this could be considered giving any aid and comfort to the enemy, but as I expected to *get* some aid and comfort *from* the enemy in return, I thought one would balance the other. When Bill came in I told him about the chance I had and asked him what was best to do. "Well," said he, "if I could play the fiddle and had the same chance I would show you how blamed quick I would take it, but," said he, "I will miss you and I am sorry to have you go."

Shortly after, the Adjutant came up and I told him I would go with him. Before leaving the prison, the Adjutant took my parole of honor that I would not go beyond the limits of the prison without permission, and intended to bind me to do no act that would be hurtful to the interests of the C.S.A., but as he read the oath to me from the U.S. Army Regulations and confined himself very closely to the text, it was so hard to tell what he had sworn me to that I felt afterwards at liberty to construe it as suited me best; at any rate I was only an enlisted man, and in the army it is only the officers who are supposed to have honor, so my parole of honor was subject to so many doubts

Being paroled

and uncertainties that it could not stand the strain afterwards when subjected to pressure. It was dusk when we approached the Colonel's quarters and when the Adjutant presented me to the Colonel, the Colonel looked at me pretty closely and turning to the Adjutant asked, "Is he a nigger?" "Oh, no," said the Adjutant, "his hide is white enough if you once get down to it." The Adjutant then had a tub of water brought, and handing me a piece of soap told me to give myself a good scrubbing so as to be as presentable as possible. I set vigorously to work, and with the aid of the soap I soon had the greater part of the soot scrubbed off; at any rate, I was in shape to successfully establish my claims to being a white man. A fiddle was now produced and I was asked to give them a specimen of my skill. I played an old German waltz which seemed to particularly please the Adjutant, and as I knew it only by a number, No. 10, it was decided that it should be known thereafter as the Adjutant's waltz, and so it was.

After playing a few pieces, the Colonel excused me and told the Adjutant to get me some supper and have me come back later in the

Presented to Col. Iverson

evening. The Adjutant took me to the hospital bakery to get me some bread, and there I met an old acquaintance in the person of Pap Mason, a Massachusetts man by birth but for many years a resident of Bardstown, Ky., whose acquaintance I had formed inside, and whom for some time I had missed. He was assisting the bakers. The boss baker gave me a couple of the hospital wheat-flour loaves which were about the size of good big biscuits, and I lost no time sailing into them. They were good—I can't tell you how good they were, and how I enjoyed them. This bakery was a great institution and the fame of it had gone out all over the country. Ladies came from a great distance and in considerable numbers to see the Yankee bakers and their wonderful bread made without yeast. The bread was made with salt rising, and it was as beautiful bread as I ever saw, and the best bread I ever tasted. I tasted more of it that night than I ever did afterwards in any one day. One of these biscuits or hospital loaves was considered a day's ration. With the two given me by the Adjutant's order, Pap Mason managed to slip me another before I got away. I hid this inside my shirt, and whenever the chance presented itself, I slipped my hand in and broke off a piece. This disappeared before a great while and left me with a feeling in the region of my stomach that I had not experienced in many a day.

I reported, as directed, at the Colonel's quarters in the early part of the evening, but before going there indulged myself in walking around and seeing what the outside of the prison looked like. The sense of freedom was so novel that I could not realize it. Was it possible that I was outside and not subject to being starved or ill treated, or being frozen on the cold days and nights? Could it be that I had had such a glorious feed and such elegant wheat bread? I could not take it all in; it seemed too much like a beautiful dream. The feeling of freedom was more intense on the following morning, as I got a chance to see the country around and to feel that I was not hemmed in by the hateful stockade walls. I cannot describe it, and you who have never been deprived of your liberty cannot understand it. I found Collins Thompson waiting for me at Headquarters, and I learned from him how I came to be taken out. He had the run of the prison in and out for a long time, and was in the quarters of the 1st Rhode Island [Artillery] the evening I played there. The fiddler

who had been taken out when I refused to go had the misfortune a
few nights before to get hold of some pine top whiskey down at the
village, where he had been taken by the officers to play at a dance,
and before they had fairly got to dancing he was uproariously drunk,
and came near cleaning out the local confederacy. The result was,
he was bounced into the stockade very unceremoniously that very
night. The officers were bent on having a good time, but they had
no fiddler, and dancing don't amount to much unless there is a fiddle connected with it.

At this juncture, Thompson told the Adjutant about me and
urged him to bring me out. The Colonel consented, although I don't
think he cared much about music or dancing either. I *know* he did
not entertain a very high opinion of fiddlers, from a conversation I
had with him afterwards. He said to me on that occasion, "Ripley"
(the rebels never seemed to grasp the subtleties of my name) "what
did you work when you were home?" I answered, "I kept a drug store
before I enlisted." "Is that so," he answered, "why, that is quite a respectable business. I didn't suppose you were of much account because you played the fiddle; the fellows down here who play the fiddle are no-account fellows, and nobody thinks much of them." I tried
to explain to him that we had some very respectable fiddlers, up
north, and that it was not an uncommon thing to find doctors,
lawyers, merchants, and even ministers who played the fiddle, not
always for dances, however.

I had a good many conversations with Col. Iverson during the
short time I was outside, and I found him a gentleman, a kind-
hearted though high-tempered man and a thorough rebel. I never
knew him to use a profane word, and on occasions when his temper
would be raised, the strongest expression I ever knew him to use was
the term "grand rascal." That with him meant as much as volumes
of profanity would have meant. He considered all Yankees grand rascals to start with but some were more grand than others. He always
treated me very kindly except on one occasion to which I will refer
hereafter.

I found one of the 16th Conn., a German by the name of Peter
Grohman at the Colonel's quarters, and we tried a few pieces together.[18] He played the guitar quite well, and being a German, he had

no difficulty in playing accompaniments to the German waltzes, polkas, and gallops which kept coming to the surface as I played. In front of the Colonel's quarters, nearly the entire military force of the camp was collected, listening to our music. I gained many friends among the rebel soldiers by my playing. They were great lovers of music, and many of them told me that they had never heard much music in their lives, except banjo music. The first night's entertainment was quite a success, judging by the attention of the audience. After the concert I made my way to the bakery again and by some sleight-of-hand performance of Pap Mason's, I got away from there with two more loaves inside my shirt. The exercise of the evening enabled me to stow away one loaf without any particular difficulty, but the fifth loaf was not so easily disposed of. I was full to the chin, but the desire to eat was as great as at the first; it seemed as if I could not eat enough. I would eat more as soon as I had room until I could hardly breathe. I had no comfort sitting or lying down. The only relief I could get was in walking around. Somewhere about midnight I got the last of the fifth loaf packed away, and somewhere between that and morning, I got so I could take a long breath. It was a most fortunate thing that it was not solid food or it would surely have killed me; as it was, I felt uncomfortable for some time afterwards. The next day, Thompson told me that the officers were so well pleased that they wanted us to get up a string band.

We found, on looking around, a very good flute player by the name of Barber, of an Iowa regiment (Barber had with him a little flying squirrel that had been his companion all through his imprisonment. He captured it during the Battle of Kennesaw Mt., when it was scarcely bigger than a mouse, and carried it in his blouse pocket always after that. It would run around his shoulders and perch itself on his head, eat out of his hand, and at the approach of anyone would dart into his master's pocket, and from there would peek out in all directions. It would not make friends readily with strangers and would nip sharply anyone who attempted any liberties. Running in and out of the blouse pocket had worn the hair off his tail, until it was just like a rat's tail.) Thompson was able to play a very good second violin and with the two violins, flute, and guitar, we had a respectable orchestra. Thompson was a real genius, and seemed to be

The Orchestra

able to do anything he chose to try. He could play the violin, and, to our surprise, took up the guitar one day and demonstrated that he could beat Pete Grohman out of sight as a guitar player. The guitar we had belonged to a lady in the neighborhood, and there was probably not another nearer than Charleston or Wilmington.

Thompson made the remark that if he could get strings he would make a guitar. We thought he was only bragging, but in a short time he came around and said the officers had told him to go ahead and make the guitar and they would get the strings. He started in and I accompanied him. He went down in the swamp, cut a nice straight grained ash tree, cut out a block of proper thickness, split out a couple of sections next to the center, and then kiln-dried them at the ovens at the bakery until they were as thoroughly seasoned as he could get them, then worked them down with a drawing knife to the proper thickness; went down into the swamps again and dug laurel roots for the keys, worked the frets and nuts cut of bone, and last and most wonderful of all made the glue to glue it.

When it came to gluing the guitar we found no glue was to be had in or about Florence. Thompson got permission to go to the slaughter-house to get some cattle hoofs to make glue of, and along with the hoofs we got an ox heart from Russell, the rebel sergeant of the butcher's squad. Pap Mason baked the heart for us in the bread oven. Thompson boiled the hoofs down until he had reduced them to the proper consistency, and when we got through we had enough glue to glue all the guitars in South Carolina. By the time the guitar was ripe and ready for use, the officers had succeeded, at an expenditure of $250.00, in getting the strings. The varnish was procured of our old friend the negro car-builder. Everything belonging to the guitar except the strings had been manufactured and put together by Thompson, and when it was finished and strung up, it was better in tone than the other guitar. It was about this time that Charleston was being evacuated, and the rebel sergeant who bought the strings brought also a canteen of old peach brandy, for which he had paid the same as he had for the strings. He did me the honor to offer me a drink of it, and I, oblivious of the great distinction of drinking peach brandy worth $700.00 a gallon, actually refused, to the great surprise and disgust of Sergeant Bush, who could only say as he drew the canteen down from his lips, "Well, you are the doggonedest fool I ever did see."

This Sergeant Bush was a character himself. I never saw anything particularly out of the way in his dealings with our men, but he had a bad name. It was said that prior to the war his business was stealing negroes in one state and selling them in another. Of course the abolition of slavery ruined his business. When drunk he was treacherous and ugly. I saw him draw has revolver one night, cock it, and hold it to the head of one of his brother sergeants and threaten to blow his brains out if he would repeat a certain remark he had made. The other man said to him as coolly as if there was no revolver in question at all, "Bush, you are too big a coward to shoot me, you are too big a coward to shoot anybody that has anything themselves to shoot with. You know yourself, you are a coward, and I know you are a thief. If you don't take that revolver down and put it away in less than a quarter of a minute I will ram it down your throat." Bush gave a little laugh, uncocked it, and returned it to his belt. For a few min-

Refusing a drink of peach brandy

utes the other sergeant gave a brief but comprehensive biography of the most contemptible villain that ever went unhung, and he said he went by the name of Bush, but it wasn't his right name, and Bush with all his bluster dare not resent it, although the other man was unarmed. The rebel sergeants at Florence were a good lot of men, with the exception of Bush.

We had now first and second violin, flute, and guitar, and we were prepared to gratify the officers as far as their dancing was concerned, except that we yet lacked a prompter, to us a seeming necessity, but of not so much importance as we afterwards learned to them. We soon filled this want by one who was himself an excellent dancer, as well as prompter. I also succeeded in getting a friend out of prison to play violin for us. He could not play much but he could go through the motions in a manner that would deceive almost anyone. His real name was John H. Crawford, and he was from Ohio, but he was known in and out of prison as Jake Lippard.[19] I heard from him a few years ago. He took up music on his return home and now follows it for a living. He was a good singer and helped us more in that way than with the violin. In all my prison experience I never met a better fellow than Jake Lippard. Our musical association was strengthened by the addition of another Ohio man by the name of Kimball. He was really an officer, and as such should not have been with us according to the prison rules. When captured he had on a private's blouse and pants and so was turned in with the rest.[20]

Kimball was a born leader. When the sanitary goods came through he was selected from among the prisoners to assist in their distribution, and when that was concluded was retained on the outside to do office work. I think Col. Iverson thought a great deal of him, and no man of us would express our opinions to the Colonel as freely as he would. One morning, after a number of prisoners had tunneled out and been recaptured, and the dogs and cowboys had had a lively chase in getting them, the Colonel, happening to pass Kimball, could not keep from venting a little of his displeasure on him, he being the handiest object, and said, "Kimball, you Yankees are all grand rascals, and if I had my way I would hang every Yankee in the South today." The Colonel said more than he meant, but Kimball was a match for him. Said he, "Colonel Iverson, you and I think about alike on this matter. If I had my way, I would hang every damned rebel from the Potomac to the Gulf." It was too much for Iverson. He turned away from Kimball and went to his quarters without saying a word back, but he was heard to say to one of his officers, "I believe that rascal Kimball would do what he says if he could."

There was always a crowd of negroes in front of the quarters where we were practicing, and I never knew any persons to show such genuine appreciation as they did. To them the guitar was never anything but a species of banjo, and they would never call it anything else. Thompson would sometimes take the guitar instead of the fiddle and he would throw himself into all sorts of attitudes and shapes and imitate turning the crank of a hand organ while he was playing, and his contortions would get the negroes so wild with pleasure that they could hardly contain themselves, they would pat for dear life, in time to the music. One day one fellow, after listening to and watching Thompson for some time, broke out with "'Fore God I'd give de

whole state of Souf Carliny if I could play the banjo like dat dar man."
The negroes were not much more attentive to our playing than were
the guards. They were around our quarters in dozens nearly all
the time.

We were notified one day soon after this that we would be taken
down to the village to serenade some ladies that evening, and we
should prepare ourselves for it. I found it necessary to make some
repairs in my wardrobe. I was in the most disreputable shape of anyone in the orchestra. From someplace, Jake Lippard got me a pair
of cavalry breeches which fitted me very well and were much warmer
than the old ones from which I parted with no regrets, although we
had been such inseparable companions for so many months. My old
blouse was minus one sleeve and part of the tail, and someone produced its counterpart minus the other sleeve, and part of the back,
thus making one tolerably good blouse out of the two. I had my slip-
pers yet, or what remained of them, but had no socks and none were
to be had. One of the rebel sergeants, a very companionable and intelligent fellow about my own age, had become quite intimate with
me. He could talk about the war without getting mad, and although
I was a prisoner, he would listen patiently to my views and give me a
respectful hearing no matter how much he might disagree with me.
Of all my rebel acquaintances, I never met one for whom I had a
stronger regard. I regret very much that both his name and the name
of his home have escaped my memory. He, learning that a pair of
socks were needed to make me presentable, came to me and insisted
on my taking a pair of his which he had just received from home. In
fact, he only had one other pair. He was a good fellow and I would
like to meet him again. The socks would have been a curiosity if you
could have seen them. By this time, February, 1865, the Southern
people were compelled to utilize everything and anything in the way
of clothing, and these socks were knit out of cotton store cord. They
did feel about the nicest thing in the world, though, on my sore and
swollen feet.

I was now well equipped for the serenade, and at early dusk, under charge of several of the officers, we proceeded to the village. We
made our first halt and opened our serenade in front of a mansion
with tall white pillars situated in a grove of southern pines. As we com-

Presented with a pair of socks

menced to play, it started the dogs up in opposition in all directions far and near, and it had the same effect on the negroes, for before we had gotten half through the first piece we were surrounded by all the negroes belonging to the plantation. After playing a few pieces we were invited into the house and given seats in the broad hallway. In the sitting room, which we could see from where we sat, was an old-fashioned fire-place, and with its big logs ablaze it looked very comfortable and inviting indeed. On every step of the broad and long stairway leading from the main entrance upstairs, the little negroes were clustered and such an audience as we had. It was one of the most amusing things I ever witnessed. It made no difference to them what we played. They patted and danced just as well to "Annie Laurie" as they did to "Way Down South in Dixie," and they danced [to] everything. There were no restrictions placed on our selection of pieces, and we played what we chose, among other things, the "Star-Spangled Banner." I had played it many times in my life before, sometimes as a solo, sometimes in orchestra, and sometimes with the voice, but I never played it for a dance before.

The Serenade

Before leaving, we were treated to a piece of cake by one of the ladies, and she explained that they had no sugar for cakes now, and were obliged to use sorghum instead. We begged her not to feel worried about a little thing of that kind, as we were not particular. It was not the particular ingredients that worried our minds, it was whether the supply would equal the demand or not. These latter remarks were not made to the young lady, however, but among ourselves, for while we were treated kindly we were not placed on a conversational footing. Our playing was very satisfactory, and the officers were complimented on the excellence of their string band. We returned to camp in good order about midnight, and on the way there, elated by the success of our first appearance in public, a winter campaign was planned in which we were to have an active part.

Through the violin I got on very intimate terms with nearly all the rebel officers and sergeants; of some I have already spoken; of some others I will speak briefly. As I recollect now, the officers of the prison were as follows: Lt. Col. Iverson, 55th Ga., Commandant; Lt.

The Concert

Cheatham, Adjutant; Lt. Wallace, Quartermaster; Capt. Butler; Lt. Lane; Lt. Barrett; Lt. Wilson [the last five listed as "Officers on duty"]; Sergt. Russel; Sergt. Beacham; Sergt. Bush.[21]

Lt. Lane was an officer with whom I did not get much acquainted. He had lost an arm in the service; was tall and one of the most soldierly appearing of the officers. As far as I knew, he was kind to the prisoners, as far as he had anything to do with them. Lt. Wilson was a Marylander; he had been wounded in the right elbow at Gettysburg and his arm had to be carried in a bent shape. He got a new uniform by the blockade about the time I got out, and was the most gorgeously appareled officer at the post. The Confederate officer's uniform was a very handsome uniform when new and well made, and of the regular Confederate grey. Lt. Wilson when sober was generally very touchy and cross, but as he was only sober at long intervals and then only for a short time, we knew him mostly under the influence of Pine Top or Sorghum seed whiskey. When his clay was tolerably well moistened, he could outswear any man in the Confederate army, and he used to stand on the stockade embankment, and just let himself loose on occasions. I think he suffered a great deal with his arm and drank to deaden the pain. I never knew him to do anything worse to a prisoner than to swear at him, and then he would swear just as freely at one of his own soldiers. The soldiers were not hard swearers as a rule, but occasionally you would find one who would make up for what the others lacked. Lt. Wilson was kind-hearted with all his failings, and he became a good friend of mine. Capt. Butler was an older man than any of the others, and a very tall and strongly built man. He had considerable fun in him and talked very freely with us about the war. His hobby was the recognition of the Confederacy by foreign powers. Every week he would have this in some different form for our information and amusement.

The Quartermaster, Lt. Wallace, was a rougher man than any of the others. A pretty level-headed man, I think; a rebel of rebels, although he was said to be of Northern birth. I did not have much to do with him, but those of our boys who did, spoke pretty well of him. I now come to one of whom I find it impossible to say one word of praise, or for whom to offer one word of excuse. A braggart and a bully when armed, among unarmed men his general style and manner made me believe he was a coward at heart. He was Lt. Barrett, and he was known throughout the prison as a redheaded devil. I do not believe he had ever been at the front, for he did not have any of the characteristics of a man who had seen service. Among all the prisoners who ever saw him, I have yet to find one who could say a good word for him. He would take delight in torturing men and witnessing their agonies. He would cut off the rations for a fancied offense. He would come to the gate about time to distribute the rations for the day, when hundreds would be waiting in front of the gate, and in a tone of voice that could not be heard one quarter of the way through the dense throng would order them back, and then if the order was not promptly obeyed, as it was oftentimes impossible to do, so great was the pressure behind, would draw his revolver and with a savage oath fire into the midst of the crowd. His ambition, as he told, was to make the Yanks afraid of him. It did not have this effect, but it made us hate him. The diabolical acts of this inhuman monster were too numerous and too horrid to recount. He was a fit

Lt. Barrett firing on the prisoners

instrument of the master devil, General Winder, who no doubt prized him as one who was ready and willing to carry out his hellish schemes.

Of the sergeants, there was Russell, who had charge of the butcher's squad. He was a splendid fellow and our men who were under him could not say too much for him. Sergeant Frank Beacham of Cuthbert, Ga., was another fine fellow, and one who was uniformly kind to the prisoners. There was another young fellow whose name I have forgotten; he was only a boy and his father was a prominent man in the State of Georgia. I learned one tune, "Billy on the Low Grounds," from him which he whistled for me until I learned it; and he was very proud of his tune and never failed to call for it when I played for him, or played where he was. Of the soldiers, I came to know a great many, and I found a number of them Union men who had been conscripted and brought into service at the point of the bayonet. The bayonet is a wonderful persuader. I was persuaded once to hurry into a car at the sharp end of a bayonet, and I have never forgotten the feeling.

The rebel soldiers were full of curiosity and were very credulous. That they could fight well there is no disputing, but I do not see how they could be managed and maneuvered in mass, for there seemed to be no idea among them of drill or discipline. I never saw them drilling all the time I was on the outside of the prison. All they did was to have guard mount every morning, and such a guard mount. They could hardly stay in line to be counted, and I never heard them complete a count of their own accord in my life. The guard mount was held just in front of Headquarters and I had good opportunities to see it. One morning during guard mount it happened that there were no rebel officers in Headquarters, and a number of paroled men were in there. The guard line was facing from Headquarters. Kimball, standing in the door, said, "Now, boys, I want you to watch that line; I will bet that inside of five minutes I will have the entire line looking back here instead of to the front." He had a small spring tape measure, a novelty to probably nine-tenths of the rebels in camp, many of them possibly never had seen one. He leaned carelessly against the sides of the door, and fixing his eyes on some faraway object, he began to draw out the tape and then touch the spring and let it fly back. The unusual unaccountable noise in the rear caused a rebel soldier to look back to see what it was. Here was a mystery; he nudged his neighbor and they wondered together. Kimball apparently oblivious of what was going on kept up his work, and every time the tape flew back, another recruit was gained. Lt. Lane wanted his guard to count off, but it was impossible to get their attention and he stormed up and down the line, almost beside himself with vexation. Kimball had the floor and he kept it until he had made his promise good. I do not think there was a man in the line who did not come around sometime during the day to see that doggoned thing that Kimball was shooting off at guard mount.

Chapter Six

The keeping of the prison records, the baking for the hospital, the attendance on the sick, the butchering for the camp, the wood chopping, and the burying of the dead were all done by our own men. No work of service, however, that properly belonged to the Confederate Army was performed by any of them. If our men had not performed the offices above, they probably would not have been performed at all, or would have been done in a very indifferent manner and we would have suffered for it, for aside from the fact that they did not have the force to do the work, they did not have the intelligence or ability to do it well. One of the principal attendants in the hospital was John Garvey, a West Virginian.[22] He was a wagon master, I think, of a construction train, and was not in the U.S. service when captured, but he had to come in with the rest of the boys. Garvey was an excellent man in the hospital, and also was a great hand at smuggling things through to the inside of the prison. Col. Iverson was informed that a great deal of stuff was getting into prison in some way and it seemed impossible to tell by what channel or in what way. He became convinced after a while that it must be through the hospital. Garvey was warned to be careful, that the Colonel was on his track, and he took the hint. No evidence could be discovered against Garvey, and yet the work went on. The Colonel appeared very suddenly in the hospital one day, and encountered Garvey with a small bag of meal passing through. He at once accused Garvey of passing things through the prison, but he stoutly denied it and appeared to be so hurt by the unjust suspicion that he finally convinced the Colonel that his suspicions were unjust and unfair.

The Colonel left him with the remark, "Garvey, I did think you were a grand rascal, but you seem to be able to disprove it, and I guess you're all right." Garvey very fervently thanked the Colonel and moved away about his business. In the bag of meal in his hand were a dozen eggs which he was smuggling through for the boys inside.

Pap Mason was quite a ventriloquist, and the evening's entertainment would sometimes include some samples of his skill which resulted in giving the old man quite a reputation as a wizard. He would imitate sawing wood and the buzzing of a bee, and would throw his voice up the chimney and hold a conversation with some imaginary rebel up there. This was the crowning feature of the evening's entertainment, and elicited great applause. The old man got the fever shortly after I came out and died in the latter part of February.

The prisoner in charge of the burial squad was named Mitchell, and he belonged to a New Jersey regiment. The matter of burial in Florence was the same as in Andersonville; a trench was dug 3 or 4 feet deep, 6 1/2 to 7 feet in width, and 100 feet or more in length. In

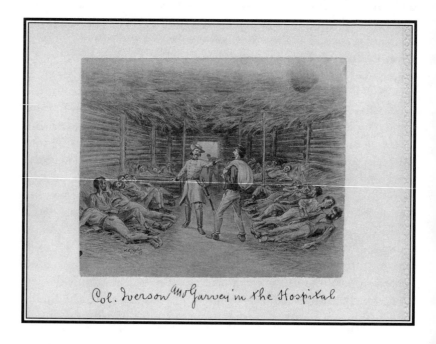

Col. Iverson and Garvey in the Hospital

this the dead would be laid side by side, and covered over with sand. A rive would be placed at the head of each body and driven down with the number as it would appear on the death record cut on it. Mitchell realized that the death record of Florence prison would someday be a valuable record to have, and about the time I came out commenced to make a copy of it for himself. I assisted him at times, and between us we copied the entire death record, and continued it up to the last man who was buried there. A fatality seems to have attended the records of this prison. The original records were lost in some way, and never came to light. When we got to Wilmington, and were exchanged, Mitchell was taken with the prison fever. He was so sick that we were unable to take the vessel we first intended to take to Annapolis, Md., and I would not leave without him, as we had been close friends and comrades. This vessel was burned at sea the second day out, and nearly 700 exchanged prisoners were lost.[23] Had I given away to my eagerness to get home and have deserted my comrade, I would probably have been lost with the rest. We went the following day and Mitchell was so sick, we had to carry him aboard. When we arrived at Annapolis he was taken to the hospital and everything belonging to him, the records among the rest, were placed on the stretcher by his side on the dock. During his illness they were lost, and I believe today there are no records in existence of this prison, where 2,800 prisoners died in the short space of five months.

While copying the records, a large number of letters came through the lines for prisoners at Florence. I think they all came by the way of Richmond, where they had all been examined and endorsed. There were a great many for whom there were no claimants. Those for whom they were intended had passed beyond the lines into "Fame's eternal camping ground," some of them months before. I preserved one such, addressed to Charles F. Stewart of the 97th New York, and endorsed on it the names of a number of my friends who had died there, with the numbers of their graves as they appeared on the death record, with the date of death, and this simple record had been instrumental in each case, in obtaining for the widows and orphans, the pensions which they so much needed.[29]

The great hope of the rebels at this time lay in the recognition of the Confederacy by foreign powers. It was their constant theme, and

as the time passed on and Savannah fell, and Charleston was evacu-
ated, and Sherman began to tighten his coils around them, and they
saw their last hopes fading away, they began to show evidences of
their loss of hope; but they were too good grit to acknowledge it. We
could not get any news from the officers at all. They maintained a
discreet silence on all subjects in our hearing. But not so their slaves,
their servants, and the negroes in the vicinity. They were always willing to tell, and so perfect a system of telegraphy had they throughout the Confederacy that they would know of Sherman's movements and operations long before the official news would get to the
officers. We knew of the burning of Columbia, through the negroes,
some hours before word was received at Headquarters. Each day we
were kept informed of the condition of the advance and the movements of our troops to confront Sherman.

The Southern slave was a shrewd fellow; it was hard to catch him
off his guard. He appeared dull and unobservant and only bent on
getting along as easy as he could through life. He was not interested
in anything in particular if there was a rebel within sight or hearing,
but get him somewhere where he knew he was safe, and he could
talk without reserve, and that negro would be as full of news as a Sunday edition of the *New York World*. His news was very reliable too;
sometimes a little off with regard to numbers, for they could not
count or calculate numbers of men worth a cent, but we knew
enough of that characteristic to discount it, so as to get at the truth.

Having free range of the outside of the prison, I took advantage
of it to scout around considerably. I was much embarrassed, however,
by not having any spectacles. I one day came across the kennel where
the dogs were kept, which were used to track the escaped prisoners.
There were over twenty in this pack, I was told, although there were
not many there the day I saw them. It is a mistake to call these dogs
hounds. I never saw any bloodhounds at Florence. These were black
dogs. They were not generally very large, although there were four
or five good-sized ones in this pack. They were generally about the
size of ordinary fox hounds. These dogs were trained to follow a
man's track and to attack him when they came up with him. They
were not fed any meat and their scent was keen, and when they
caught and tackled a prisoner and got a taste of blood, they were very

fierce. I don't know how much worse bloodhounds might be, but I question whether they would be any more savage or tenacious than these dogs were. The little negro who kept them bore a great many scars where they had nipped him, and he had to be very careful of himself with them. He used to go with them on the track, and used a peculiar howl to set them on the track that you could hear as far as you would hear the dogs.

The fame of our orchestra, and the Yankee bread, spread through the surrounding country, and many ladies came to the prison to see the bread baked by the prisoners and hear the music by the Yankee string band. They came in wagons and carts and nondescript vehicles, drawn by old, broken-down horses, mules, oxen, and cows. The Confederacy was getting at mighty low ebb about this time. The ladies, some of them, were dressed in silks, the relics of former days, but all showed the marks of pinching poverty and great need in their apparel. We were always glad to see them. Not that we had the opportunity to enjoy their company or conversation particularly, but it almost always happened that after playing for them, and they got ready to go, we would fall heir to what extra sweet potatoes they might have. These were much to be desired, and we desired them. They appeared to like our music but did not seem particularly impressed with our appearance. It is mighty hard to brace up and put on any style when your hair is leaking through the roof of your hat, and your feet are clad in old cloths or fragments of shoes, and you haven't changed your shirt in six months, and your attenuated limbs are seen in all their bony symmetry through the verandas in your pantaloons. A man may stand up and make the best of such combinations, but he can hardly appear interesting or impress favorably by his appearance.

We made frequent visits to the village with the officers. One evening soon after our serenade, we went down to play for a dance. Nearly all the officers were with us. We were allowed considerable freedom this evening, and when we were not playing, we mixed quite freely in the crowd, always avoiding the ladies. Jake Lippard got to talking with the negro women and they had a great curiosity to know "whar he kept his hohns." They said, "Why, dey tell us you uns, Yanks has got hohns on your heads, but we don't see um." Jake assured them that we all had them originally, but they had all done got knocked off, standing on our heads. Jake had a wonderful lot of fun with them. When the dancing first commenced, our prompter tried to form them in sets so as to dance a quadrille, but they did not seem to take readily to it. After playing two or three sets, a young boy came to me and asked, "What is that Yank hollerin' about?" "Why," I said, "he is calling the figures of the dance," and tried to explain what it meant. "Oh," he said, "he needn't bother with that, they don't know or care about dancing, they want to dance to suit themselves," and so they did, anywhere from six to thirteen in a set, and dancing as they chose, and the little negroes were mixed through them dancing away for dear life.

Lt. Wilson succumbed to the heat of the room and the strength of the "pine top" early in the evening, and after being assisted to a seat, by his lady, relapsed into a condition of innocuous desuetude from which he did not rally until the dance was over. In one of the intervals of the dance I went into the room where the gentlemen were having liquid refreshments, and I was offered a drink by the young son of the host, which I refused, thanking him for the offer. He was thunderstruck. Was it possible; was it because I was afraid of the liquor? "No, I don't drink," I said. This was a puzzle. "Here, you uns, look heah, heah's a Yank that don't drink whiskey." I was the subject of considerable comment among them. I knew then for the only time in my life wherein lay the glory of being the most prominent temperance man in the country. I was not only the most prominent, but in fact the only temperance man in the house that night.

Each day brought us news of the approach of Sherman. We could see the rebels were nervous and anxious, and we began to be anxious too. They began to make preparations that looked like moving us away. There was a Michigan man, an attendant at the hospital by the name of Marvin Bogart.[25] He was a cool, brave fellow, and very quick to judge what the movements of the Johnnies meant. He and Kimball used to run across each other, apparently accidentally very often, would pass a few words, and carelessly stroll away from each other again. One day Kimball said to me, "Would you like to go back into the stockade again?" I answered, "No, indeed, I would not." "Well," said he, "there is where you are going very soon. It is where

The Virginia Reel

we are all going; not in this stockade, for Sherman will soon break this up, but in some other stockade, maybe Salisbury. You know what that means." I knew what going into the stockade meant, and I had no intention of going back again if it could be helped. "Well," said I, "what can we do? Can we get away?" "Yes," he replied, "we are making up our party, and we are nearly ready. We will probably start tomorrow night if we can get off. Provide yourself with some extra bread, and be ready when I give you the word. Don't say a word to anyone, for you don't know who can be trusted."

The nights were at their darkest now, which was very good for our purpose. The plan as unfolded to me later was as follows: Kimball and Bogart were to be the leaders. Our objective point was to be at the Peedee River, as near as we could learn, about 20 miles distant in a northeasterly direction, through the pine woods. Kimball had got around one of the rebel guards, a Union man, who showed him where he could get some guns and ammunition, and when we were ready to start, five guns were procured, the faithful rebel standing guard for us while they were stolen. They were put in the hands of the most reliable and strongest men in the party. On account of my nearsightedness, no gun was given me. There were nineteen in the party, nearly all the orchestra, the most of the clerks and some of those in whom the Colonel had the most faith, Garvey, Bogart, and several attendants among the rest.

A short time after 10 o'clock, when all the camp was still, Kimball came flitting around and gave us all notice to assemble a short distance below Headquarters on the road to the village, and that we must all be there within a few minutes, as we must start as soon as possible, and make as much distance as we could before they got the dogs on our track. I was at the appointed place in a very short time, and found most of the party already on hand. I found another thing too, which made me feel a little uncomfortable. Some of our party had got hold of some "pine top," and they were hilarious and so reckless as to endanger the success of our venture.

Just as we were ready to start, a warning "hiss" came from Kimball, and we all lay as still as if we were dead. Someone was approaching from the direction of the town. Presently two young rebels came along, very busily engaged in conversation, and passed right through the center of our party. We were lying down on each side of the road. They stopped when a few feet from us, and we thought sure we were discovered; but they started on again, and as soon as they got out of hearing we got up and started off. We were soon in the woods, keeping close together, and before long struck a road leading in the direction we wanted to go. We struck a good gait, and kept it up so long that it began to tell severely on me. I was not strong enough yet for very long, sustained exercise, and this was pretty violent. We were traveling through the pine woods, and they were so dense and the trees so close and high that it was as dark as it was possible for it to be. Our eyes got somewhat accustomed to the darkness, after a time, so that we could see a little distance ahead and kept trace of the road through the woods.

After traveling about three miles, we saw a light, and as we approached the house heard someone singing. We knew it was a negro's cabin, and one of the party went to the house to get information about the road ahead, and how far it was to the ferry. I forgot to mention before that our plan was to get to the ferry, cross over in the boat, and then cut it loose or disable it, and with the river between us and our pursuers, to keep us off with the guns, and make our way down the other side of the Peedee River, to Bulls Bay on the coast, where we were informed our troops had landed and taken possession a few days before. It was a tramp of over a hundred miles through a wild and unknown wilderness, and if we had even crossed the river, there would have been about one chance in ten of our making it. Our scout learned that we were on the direct road, and that it was about thirteen miles to the ferry. As I said before, figures did awfully bother the negroes, they were utterly unreliable on the question of numbers and figures, and if we had gone on three miles further and found another one, he would have been very likely to have told us that it was fifteen miles from there to the ferry.

We started along again but at a reduced rate, for we were none of us able to keep up the strain. After traveling as I thought, two or three miles further, we halted for a short rest, and a conference, and to count up to see if all were there. One was missing—a barber named Dang, but it was thought he would catch up to us in a short time, and even if he did not, we dared not wait for him. When the order was given to march again, I started with the rest, but I felt so tired and faint that I felt myself obliged to sit down again before I had gone very far. I told the boys nearest me to go on and I would follow as soon as I was rested a little more, and I would try to overtake them before they got to the ferry. I never felt so lonesome in my life as when they got out of hearing. The silence was so oppressive, it could be felt. Instead of feeling better, however, I kept feeling worse, and when I attempted to get up and follow the others, I found I could scarcely stand.

While I was attempting to pull myself together, I heard something that put life into me but banished hope of escape. In those pine woods you can hear a great distance on a quiet night. Away off as far as I could hear, I could distinguish the first notes of our dreaded enemy, the hounds. The first sound that came to me was the howl of the driver urging them on the chase. Then came the deep bay of the older and leading dogs, followed by the yelps of the smaller ones. All at once I heard the whole pack in unison. I knew they had struck our trail. I had not looked for their getting our track so soon, for we thought after discovering our absence they would have to circle around the prison with the dogs before they struck our track, and that ought to give us a good three hours start. In the first place our absence was accidentally discovered a little earlier than we expected and the camp was aroused, and just as the search was about being made throughout the quarters, Quartermaster Wallace laid his hands on Dang, the barber, who, with his blanket tied around him, had just come, and was trying to sneak to his quarters. He had become frightened and had concluded to back out by the time we got to our first resting place, possibly before, and was trying to get back to camp unobserved. Putting a rope around Dang's neck and throwing it over a beam of the Headquarter's shanty, he (the quartermaster) told him to tell instantly which way the others had gone or he would hang him. A slight tightening of the rope overcame any hesitation Dang might have had, and he at once told the quartermaster all he wanted to know. The dogs were all ready and were at once put on the track, and the chase began. There is all the difference in the world in chasing and being chased.

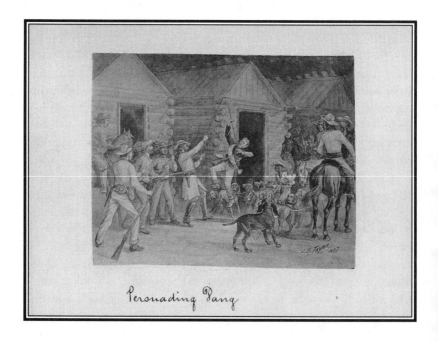

Persuading Dang

As the distant bay of the hounds came to my ears, I forgot my lameness and exhaustion for the instant, and I sprung to my feet. My impulse was to follow after my comrades, but after taking a few steps in that direction, I began to realize that it would be folly to do this with the dogs on my track. They would overhaul me before I could possibly overtake the others, and would tear me to pieces before the cavalry could get up with them. I thought quick. It was no time for lengthy deliberations. On the right side of the road, the ground was dry and the trees were all pine, straight as arrows, and from twenty to forty feet before there would be a limb. On the lower side, at some distance from the road, there was a swamp through which ran a stream of water. The certainty of our being chased by the dogs and the chances that we would be overtaken were fully discussed while our plans for escape were being matured. We decided that our safest plan when pursued by them would be to avoid the dry ground, and not climb trees, but to seek the swamp, and endeavor to get to the water in order to throw them off the scent. From the experience of other prisoners who had been treed, we knew it meant our coming down when ordered down, out of the tree, among the dogs, to be torn by them, or remaining in the tree to be shot out of it. Knowing this, I decided to make for the swamp and try to gain the creek before the dogs could reach me. I could hear them all the time, coming nearer, and the howls of that little driver like an imp of hell, urging them on. Jumping as far as I could into the bushes to clear the road and break my track, I made for the swamp and creek with all haste. I soon found the swamp, but did not succeed in getting to the creek. As I worked my way farther into the swamp, the footing became very uncertain. Now a hump, and next mud to my knees; again, I would catch my toe on a root and down I would go on my face in the mud and water.

Perhaps some of you are acquainted with Carolina swamps; you may have traveled through them in daylight, but probably not by night. If you have, you know something of what dismal places they are. But you will find it very hard to convey an adequate idea of what they are to anyone who may never have seem them. Gloomy and dismal as they may be in the daytime, it gives you no idea of what they are at night. You can feel the darkness and clamminess all around you like a pall. The mortal being hunted in such a place, with the deadly moccasin snakes on all sides, and the savage dogs behind you, and behind them all, men more savage and unfeeling than the dogs, is a fate in comparison with which death on the battleground has no terror.

It was hard work in the darkness and mud. I could not make much headway, and I could hear the dogs coming nearer and nearer. At last I could go no farther; I took my station in the middle of a small group of saplings, and by standing on the networks of their roots I could keep up out of the mud. This was a great advantage to me in the fight which ensued, as the mud was soft and deep all around me. I had some hope the dogs might miss my track, or if they tried to follow me in the swamp would lose it in the thin mud and water, and that I might thus escape them. I about concluded in my own mind that my record would be finished that night, for I did not expect to get out alive. I had nothing with which to defend myself except my bare hands and feet, but I determined to make as good a fight as I could with them. I could hear the dogs very plainly now, and I knew they were drawing very close. When they came to the spot where I left the road, they all stopped their yelling as suddenly as if their wind had been shut off, but it was only for a minute. Very soon the voice of the old leader rang out as he struck my fresh track, and in an instant the whole pack was in full cry.

I knew now there was no escape, and I nerved myself for the fight. As they drew nearer to me, they ceased yelling except to give an occasional yelp, and I could hear them splashing along in the mud and water, and thrashing through the bushes. I thought over a great deal of my life in a short time, that night; one thinks fast when he is looking over the borderline of eternity. In a short time I saw the old leader coming, twisting his way through the bushes. He was a white dog with dark spots on him, and the white seemed to have a phosphorescent gleam to it, for I could distinguish it quite a distance away. The rest of the pack was close on his heels, and the growls and snarls, as they drew nearer, gave promise of what I might expect as soon as they would reach me. I still had my haversack on me, and in it were two or three of the hospital loaves. When the dogs found me they wasted no time in preliminary arrangements, but surrounded me in an instant, and commenced the fight. I used my feet to good advantage in kicking them off, and my hands were kept actively engaged in protecting my throat. The saplings and their roots were a great protection and help. They gave a solid footing, and provided something to cling to, which helped to protect me against the possibility of being dragged down. The mud being soft, the dogs sank in up to their bodies, and as they had no firm ground to spring from, this compelled them to attack me at some disadvantage.

The old white dog led the attack as he had the chase. He caught me by the left leg just above the knee, and as he did so, I caught him by the nose with my left hand and commenced kicking him in the ribs with all my might. I completely disabled him before I got through, but while I held him by the nose, another of the dogs, climbing up his body, bit me right through the upper muscle of the left arm. About the same time two dogs succeeded in fastening themselves in either leg, and this put a stop to my kicking. When the dogs first attacked me from the rear, they tore off my haversack, and the bread in it diverted the attention of some of them for a short time;

Caught by the dogs

but as there were enough paying their attention to me as it was, I did not particularly miss a dog or two more or less, who might be temporarily otherwise occupied.

I was obliged to let go my hold on the old dog's nose, to defend myself from the other dogs, which now that my legs were fast, and I could do no more kicking, were climbing over each other to get at my throat. I could feel their hot breath in my face as they would spring at me, and their jaws would come together like steel traps, snapping at me. I fought this battle over a great many times in the delirium of the prison fever which prostrated me after I got home, and many, many times after I got well did I have the horror of it all in my dreams. I do not know how long the fight continued; it could not certainly have been a great while, but it was very lively while it lasted. My clothing was almost torn off from me, and my flesh was full of ridges where their teeth had scraped me but had not broken through the skin; while from my feet almost to my shoulders, they had left their marks upon me in more or less serious bites.[26]

The cavalry men came up at last, and beat the dogs off me, and ordered me to follow them to the road. On my way out the dogs would snarl and snap at me, and it was all the men could do to keep them from fastening on me again. I got to the road more dead than alive, covered with mud, my clothing saturated with blood, and so exhausted I could scarcely put one foot before the other. In this condition I was traveled to the camp, a distance by a short cut of probably two or three miles. A cavalryman was sent back with me, and ordering me to go ahead of his horse about a carbine length, he cocked his carbine and gave me to understand that if I undertook to get out of the road or tried to escape, he would put a hole through me. With this cheering assurance, he started me on a slow trot, and then began the hardest trial for me I ever experienced. I was barely able to raise my feet and stagger on, weak with loss of blood, and exhausted with the terrible strain of the fight with the dogs. I cannot now tell how I got back to prison. I recollect that I could not turn out to avoid the ends of the logs or stumps that would project into the road, but would strike them and tumble over them. My escort would encourage me to raise up and try it again by encouraging oaths and threats, and so it went until we reached the prison.

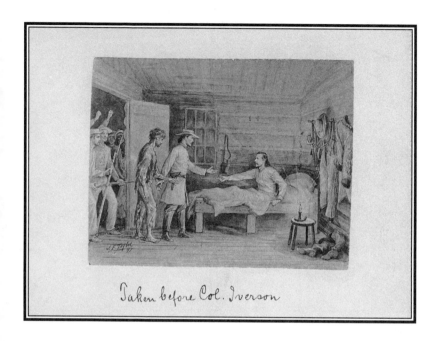

Taken before Col. Iverson

I was taken before the Colonel, who was in his quarters in bed. He sat up to listen to the accounts of my guard, and then ordered him to take me to the dungeon. This was a pen at one of the corners of the stockade, on top of which was placed one of the pieces of artillery, which commanded the prison. It was cold and wet in there, and weak and exhausted as I was, I would no doubt have died before morning had I gone in there; but to Lt. Wilson I owe a debt of gratitude, that at this moment he interceded for me, and became my security that I would not attempt to run away again. He was safe enough in that, for there was little danger of a second attempt, if I would ever recover from the first. The Colonel finally permitted me to go along with him, and he put me in one of the cabins, where it was warm and I could lie on some straw. I was so utterly exhausted, I went at once to sleep, and fought dogs and trotted ahead of cavalrymen from that time until awakened by the entrance of Lt. Wilson's servant, in the early morning, who brought me a piece of bread with butter on it. At any other time I would have gone for that bread and butter in one

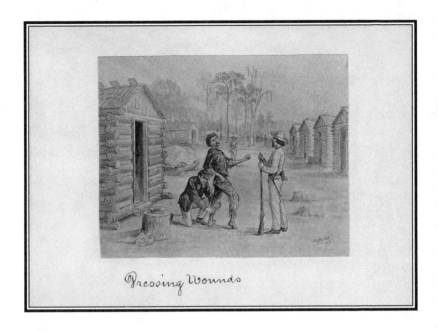

Dressing Wounds

time and two motions, as the old tactics used to say, for I had not had butter in so long, I did not know the taste of it; but I was too sick to eat it then, and so I hid it under the straw until I would feel like eating it.

When it came time to attend roll call, I hobbled out to answer to my name, and was then sent to the hospital steward to have him dress my wounds. The steward was almost entirely without remedies. He feared that unless something was done that I might get gangrene in my bites, and he powdered what appeared to me to be blue vitriol, and rubbed it freely over and in the wounds. I have already learned that a solution of blue vitriol was in common use for this purpose. It was a very severe medicine, but I think it saved my legs. My left leg in particular was badly torn, and very much inflamed. After having had my bites dressed, feeling a little hungry, I returned to the cabin to get and enjoy my bread and butter. I went to the spot where I had hidden it, but it was gone. Some fellow had been prowling around, and had found it and gobbled it. Sick and sore as I was, I forgot it all for a time. I don't think I was ever as mad in my life before or since. I did not know how badly I wanted it until it was gone. It was one of the great disappointments of my life, and although it was only a piece of bread and butter, it was something that I wanted with all my heart and soul at that particular time and place.

I met Collins Thompson afterwards at Camp Parole, Annapolis, Md., and from him got an account of the experiences of the rest of the party after they left me. The diversion caused by my capture enabled them to make better distance than they otherwise would have done. They got within about five miles of the ferry before they were overtaken by the dogs. Those who had the guns were constituted the rear guard, and they were to do what they could to stand off the rebels, and enable the others to make good their escape. They did not have much trouble in keeping the dogs back, for they could assist each other. They had provided themselves with clubs and sticks during their march. With a good club a man could make a good fight against the dogs. The dogs were always some distance ahead of the cavalry, and it was some time after the dogs reached them before the cavalry came up. Those who had the guns were posted along the road in the underbrush, and when the cavalry came up, they fired into them. The fire hurt no one, as it was very dark and they could not get aim, but it revealed their position, and the rebels poured their fire into them until they surrendered. Of the seventeen persons of the party, only twelve were brought back. Whether the other five were killed or wounded, Thompson did not know positively, but thought they must have been killed.

They returned to the prison sometime during the night, and before morning were handcuffed in pairs and put on board a train going to Wilmington. Before they got there, they overheard a conversation between a couple of rebels, which informed them of the capture of Ft. Fisher and the advance on Wilmington. The boys determined to get off the train if they died for it, and when going through the big swamp, before reaching Wilmington, they slid off the cars, handcuffed as they were, and although they were shot at by the rebel guards on the train, all fortunately escaped being hit. After lying in the swamp a day or two, they came into our lines at Wilmington, just after the surrender of the city. I slept so soundly on the night I was recaptured I did not hear them brought into camp, and I did not know of their recapture, and having been sent away to Wilmington, until told of it the next day.

Several years ago I met John H. Crawford of our orchestra, and one of those who ran away from Florence when I did, and learned some particulars of the recapture and subsequent movements of the other escaped prisoners. It was on the evening of the fourteenth of February that we ran away. We disagree as to some of the particulars. For instance, he says it was a bright, moonlit night, and my recollection is it was a dark night, and I think the facts bear me out. If it had been a bright night, we would have been discovered when the young rebs passed through our crowd just before we started. He says:

> Our party made good headway until about 2 o'clock in the morning, when we came to where the road forked and it fell to myself and one other comrade to go to some negro shanties and make inquiry in regard to which road we should take from the forks to find a flat boat on which to cross. I got the information desired at the negro quarters and reported to our leader, when we soon heard the baying of the bloodhounds behind us. In a short time they were on us, closely followed by a squad of cavalry. Some of the party climbed trees, others ran into the swamp. In a short time they had fourteen of our party together and started back to camp with us. We arrived at camp about 8 o'clock in the morning, and were marched up to Col. Iverson's headquarters, where we received a short lecture from the Colonel on Yankee insolence and were handcuffed together in pairs and put in the dungeon, where we lay for three days and nights without anything to eat or a drop of water, and so dark we could not see our hands within four inches of our faces. On the morning of the 18th we were taken from the dungeon and loaded in cars and sent to Wilmington, N.C., where we arrived on the evening of the same day. We were ferried across the Cape Fear River and camped on the bank of the Weldon Railroad just outside of the city limits. Here we got rid of our handcuffs and buried them in the sand. There was a great deal of inquiry made for the men in irons, but we disguised ourselves as best we could and were not found. On the morning of

the 21st they marched us out about twelve miles from the city in the direction of Goldsboro and camped us for the night. That night the rebels set fire to their commissary stores and also burned a large amount of rosin, tar and turpentine, and on the morning of the 22nd of February surrendered Wilmington to Generals Schofield and Terry. On the morning of the 22nd they again loaded us on the cars, and on the evening of the same day we arrived at Goldsboro, where we remained until the morning of the 26th, when we were paroled and again loaded on the cars and started in the direction of Wilmington. About noon of that day we arrived at North East River, twelve miles north of Wilmington, where we passed through the lines. I had now been a prisoner nearly eighteen months and was glad to once more find myself under the protection of the Old Stars and Stripes—long may she wave.

I find it impossible to reconcile the statements of Collins Thompson and Crawford, and other fragments which have come to me from various sources, of their movements following the time after I became separated from them. It seems to me as if their party must have become separated and each one tells the story which relates to his own party. I know I never heard that they were placed in the dungeon when they were brought back, and it seems as if I must have known it if it had been so.

Kimball was true to his character to the last. As he came to the Colonel's quarters, when brought in by the guard, he remarked to Colonel Iverson, "Colonel, I have the honor to report that your wandering minstrels have returned." He was game. I had no inclination to move around the next day at all. The pain from the bites and the soreness of my limbs and joints made me prefer to lie as still as possible. I was visited during the day by a good many of the boys, both our own and the rebels. Some of the rebels expressed much indignation that I should have been treated as I was, after having been retaken, and much to my surprise, later in the day, the cavalryman who brought me in, accompanied by Russell of the Butcher squad, came to see me. He expressed the greatest kind of regret for his rough treatment, and tried to explain that he did not know that it was me. I heard and accepted his apologies, but took very little stock in them.

I learned afterwards that his coming to apologize to me was not entirely voluntary, but was inspired by Russell's promise to thrash the ground with him if he did not do so. Russell was very kind to me at all times, and was a noble fellow, and it was generally known among the rebels that no one man had much business with him. He was very quiet and undemonstrative, and seemed always to enjoy the company of Yanks more than the rebels, although he was as thorough a rebel as any of them.

The Colonel threatened to turn us all back into the stockade next morning, that is, all the paroled men, of whom there were over a hundred on the outside. But after he got cooled down and came to consider that he could not replace us from his own force, he relented and concluded to let things go on as before. He had, however, to reorganize his force of clerks, as his most trusted ones were gone, and here my rebel friend, Lt. Wilson, came to the front again, and through his intercession I was made sergeant of the paroled men. The duties of the position were not very onerous, consisting of calling the roll and making the entries in the death record. I have my roll yet, and looking over it occasionally brings to my mind many of the old boys as they were at that time. In the *Century Magazine* of July and August 1890 is a most truthful article on prison life, written by Dr. Thos. H. Mann. His name heads the list of M's on my old roll.[27]

My string band had been robbed of its brightest stars, for Thompson, Jake Lippard, Kimball, and some others were gone, leaving only Pete Grohmann the guitar player, and Barber the flute player. My arm was so badly bitten, I could not play, so that as an organization we ceased to exist from that night. We all began to feel now that the end was drawing nigh, and that they could not hold us much longer in prison. Sherman was on his way now from Savannah, and as he advanced, the railroads were being crowded to get the cotton farther up in the country out of his way. All of the prisoners that could be removed were sent day by day to Goldsboro and Raleigh, and at last, nothing remained but the sick and dying inside, and a few paroled outside.

It was on the 26th of February, I think, that we were notified that we would leave that night for Wilmington, to be paroled and passed through the lines. This time we felt that it was true, and our hearts were so full of joy that we could not act like sane persons, but would cry and laugh and hug each other, and do the most foolish things, in our unutterable joy. Our train load that night was, perhaps, one of the happiest-feeling and saddest-looking train loads that came through to our lines. It was the cleaning up of the hospital and stockade, and the majority were almost helpless, while all the stages of misery from the ordinary to the most unspeakable were there represented. There were the gangrene cases, some with their rotting limbs, the black dead flesh separated by a distinct line from the yet sound flesh, the dead flesh in a few days to drop off and leave the white, glistening bone protruding from the flesh, and this so sensitive and painful as to draw screams of pain from them if you only touched them. Then there were those in the last stages of diarrhea, scurvy, and other complaints. It was sad and sickening, and the suffering was terrible to witness.

Four that I saw and more, I think, died on the cars before we got to Wilmington. The journey was unlike any we ever had before in the Confederacy. There was no desire to escape, no fear of the guards; a fair supply of rations, including fresh beef, had been distributed, and to those who were well enough to enjoy it, it was a picnic excursion. We talked of home and friends and what we would have to eat, and where we would go and what we would do, and we sang all the patriotic songs we knew, and we acted like school children let loose from school. I believe that if we had been disappointed at this time, it would have killed us all, so much were our hearts bound up in the one idea of getting home. I think I was the last prisoner to leave Florence. I went back to the prison after the column had started to get a bucket that I had carried with me from Andersonville (it was made out of the stockade timbers that were torn down when the prison was enlarged) and there was no one left in the camp when I came back, so that when I found the bucket and started again, I must have been the rear guard.

The afternoon before leaving, several boxes of sanitary commission goods, mostly towels, which had been standing, I do not know how long, undistributed, were broken open and distributed among us. One of the boys found a towel with a patriotic verse written on it signed by the name of a girl in his native town. There were many

Leaving Florence prison

towels with such verses written on them, and perhaps this was the reason why they had not been distributed. I got a towel and tied it
around my head. Sometime in the afternoon of the 27th our train
was stopped. This was nothing unusual, for we were obliged to make
very frequent stops. The engine, the cars, and the track were in such
poor condition that we had to run slow and stop often. One of the
boys looked out of the door towards the head of the train to see what
we were stopped for. He looked very intently for a moment, and then
more in a shriek than in his natural voice, cried out, "God, boys, it's
our pickets." And then all along the train went up a chorus of cheers
and yells. It was with difficulty we could be kept in the cars. We took
turns in going to the door to see the blue uniforms, and then we
would go to the poor, sick fellows who could not get there and try to
cheer them up. "It's all right boys, we'll soon be there, we'll soon be
in God's country again; brace up now, and you will live to see them
all at home again."

As each car was moved forward to the point of exchange, the door
would be opened, and with one of our soldiers on one side, and one

Entry into Union lines

of the rebels on the other, the order would be given to pass out, and as they passed out they would be counted by the officers. Once in their eagerness to get out, they pressed too rapidly to suit the rebel guard, and he undertook to push them back with his bayonet. As soon as he made the motion the Union soldier on the other side brought his gun down to a charge bayonet, and in language not elegant, but most expressive, warned him not to dare touch one of those men with his bayonet again. That day had gone by. While we were waiting for our turn to pass out, we had the opportunity to compare our officers and men with the rebel officers and men—the blue with the butternut. The Union officer of exchange was one of the finest-looking officers I ever saw, and he had on a beautiful new well-fitting uniform, and the contrast between him and the rebel officer was painfully apparent to the rebels themselves. The one was the soldier in the uniform of the greatest government on earth to us, the other was a traitor in the garb of dishonor. A number of the rebel soldiers took advantage of the confusion to get across the lines and get in among our men, and came to Wilmington with us.

It was touching to see with what tenderness the Union soldiers handled our sick as they were taken from the cars. It made no difference how filthy or how loathsome they were, or how contagious the disease might be, there was no hesitation, but they stepped forward and took hold of them as carefully and tenderly as if they were their own nearest and dearest friends. Oh, how good it was to be where we were esteemed worthy of decent, humane treatment again. We had been ground down so long and cruelly that we could not at first appreciate or understand. We spent the night on the other side of the Cape Fear River from Wilmington. Mitchell and I got into a Michigan regiment, and as they had been cautioned to be careful with us, and not let us have too much to eat at first, of solid food, they would not give us all we wanted at once, but gave us a little at a time. Our great desire was for fat pork, and so they gave us a small slice and some hardtack, and we set to work to cook it. It was so good, I can taste it now. It was about dusk when we got the first installment, and we got another before we lay down, and sometime in the night Mitchell nudged me, and we got up and cooked the third one.

As soon as we had breakfasted, they started us for Wilmington. As we came to the pontoon bridge over which we were to pass, I could see in the distance the Stars and Stripes flying from the steeples in Wilmington. I had not noticed them before, although we had passed through a number of camps where they must have been, and this sight of the old flag was too much for me. I had had all I could hold of joy before this came, and this was more than I could stand. On looking around among my comrades, I found that there was not one that could restrain the tears of joy that came to his eyes at the sight of the old flag. Oh, how we had learned to love it in the months that we had spent outside its protection, and how much it represented to us now. Liberty, home, friends, protection, manhood restored, civilization, God's laws and God's country, everything that was worth living for. We had attested our devotion and loyalty to it, and now we were going home to enjoy all that the supremacy of that flag would guarantee to us. I am glad that the P.O.S. of A. has undertaken to bring our children into intimate acquaintance with the old flag by having it planted on every schoolhouse in the land.[28] They cannot be taught too early their duty to it; they cannot know too much of the sacrifices of blood and life that have been offered up to preserve it to us. To none is it dearer than to those who on battlefield or in prison pen have suffered in its behalf, and the lesson that each old soldier will teach his children will be to love and revere it and with their lives preserve it from defeat or disaster.

We crossed the Cape Fear River at North East over a pontoon bridge, and as we came to the Wilmington side, we came into the camp, as I afterwards learned, of the 203rd Pennsylvania. Sheriff Asa B. Stevens of this city was in command of Company C at that time, and his headquarters were just at the end of the bridge, and he was the first officer I met, although I did not know him at the time. I presented a very dizzy appearance on my entering into Wilmington. I had no hat, the sanitary towel was tied around my head, and my hair, matted with the pine smoke of months, stood up through the towel like the plumes of a Sioux war bonnet. My blouses, of which I had to wear two to make one, hung in rags where the dogs had torn them. My pants, which were a cavalry pair, were as badly torn as my blouses, and even worse in one respect. Cavalry pants always have what is

Crossing Pontoon Bridge

called a reinforcement to protect them against the wear in riding. The dogs that night had torn this reinforcement down until it hung down like a trap door, and out of the nether end of it my long grey sanitary shirt fluttered in the breeze. My pants were tied around my ankles with ropes, and I was barefooted. Add to this the soot and smoke baked on by months of patient toil over pitch pine fires, and inability to wash it off, and you have my photograph.

As soon as we made our way to the central city, we found a line of prisoners drawing rations, and we immediately fell in line with the rest. We had had a taste of the fat pork and real coffee that our souls had yearned for so long and we wanted more of it. A sergeant stood at an open window of the Commissary building and as each one passed, he was given a big slice of bread, a slice of pork, an onion, and a pickle. Well, we just reveled in this; the onion and the pickle we had not counted on, and no apple ever tasted better or sweeter than the onion, and the pickle tasted so good that we just stayed in the line and went around and drew rations again when we came to

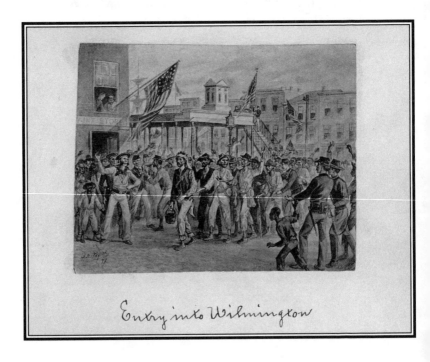

Entry into Wilmington

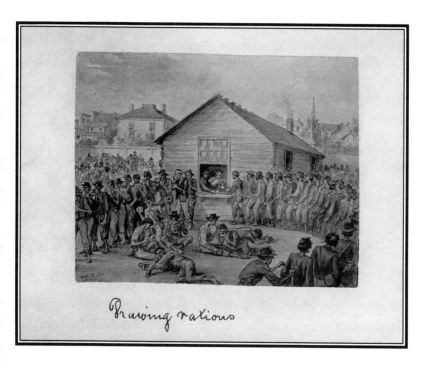

Drawing rations

the window. I think about everyone in the line made the second and some even the third and fourth visit to the window. Some of the poor fellows, though, were too far gone to enjoy the plenty which they had longed for so long. Some were too weak to stay in line, and others drew their rations and brought them to them, and after they got them, they could not eat them. They were soon picked up and taken to the hospitals. Very many died in Wilmington. The excitement had kept them up until they got inside our lines, and the reaction came, and they were too far gone to rally.

My partner Mitchell had been feeling badly all day, and he kept getting worse, and when night came was very sick. The prison fever had its clutch on him, but he was a rugged fellow, and was not disposed to give in. Every day vessels were leaving, loaded with prisoners for Annapolis, and we wanted if possible to go that afternoon, but as he did not feel well enough to stand the jam and crush getting aboard, we concluded to wait until the next morning. I have told you

On the old Transport

of the sad fate of this vessel, which we were mercifully preserved from sharing. Mitchell was no better in the morning, and we carried him aboard the vessel with us, as he would not go to the hospital and we would not leave him. We were on a slow old tub which consumed five days between Wilmington and Annapolis. We were caught in a storm off Cape Hatteras, where we tossed and rolled several days, making scarcely any headway at all. About three-fourths of those on board were sick when we started, and before we were out very long, the rest were sick also. It was a fearful place, and it was a voyage long to be remembered. The vessel was greatly overloaded, and it was a wonder we were not foundered at sea. There were not less than 750 persons aboard this boat. It was too rough to be on deck, so we were all obliged to go down in the hold. In order to give us air the sides of the boat were opened and every once in a while a high sea would dash the spray down on us. There was not a doctor nor a nurse on board, and no one to look after the very sick. For five days those who could not help themselves lay in their own filth and we all suffered from the indescribable nastiness that surrounded us. We were all more or less sick and scarcely able to help ourselves or each other. And with all this, we were crowded and packed in like sardines in a box.

On our arrival at Annapolis, Mitchell, with all his effects, was taken from the docks to the hospital. Those who were able marched up to the camp, where we were obliged to strip ourselves of all our old clothes before we were allowed to go into the building. The clothes, with their millions of Confederate lice, were burned. After undressing, we passed into a large room filled with bath tubs, large enough to hold a dozen at a time, where ready attendants scrubbed us as thoroughly as our hides would permit. It was the nicest bath I ever had in my life. The water was just warm enough to be pleasant and the scrubbing we got transformed us so that we scarcely knew each other when we got through. After our bath, we were passed into another room, where we got an entire outfit of clothes, and this so completely changed our appearance that we actually were much puzzled to

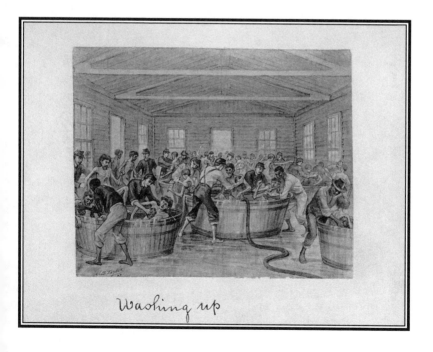

Washing up

Pressing up

recognize some of those who had been with us every day for some months past.

As soon as possible, we were mustered for pay, paid the pay, received a thirty-day furlough, and started for home, all this in one day or two. We were in God's country again, and we were the happiest lot the sun every shone on. After we got on board the cars, and I knew we were fairly started for home, I could hardly hold my head up. The cars were filled with soldiers, and they were singing "TRAMP, TRAMP, TRAMP," which had just come out, and I thought my head would split with the noise.

On my arrival at home, meeting my friends braced me up so that for a time I forgot my sickness, but when I went to bed that night, I was to remain there until the last day of my furlough, most of the time in delirium, in which the dogs, the prison, the rebel cavalrymen who took me back, and the old transport all contributed to keep me in terror and trouble night and day. Skillful treatment, gentle nursing, kind care with God's help, brought me through, and now a generation after I am permitted to recount to you what, if I had not experienced myself and known to be true, I could scarcely believe or appreciate.

I have been moderate in my statements and refrained from telling many things that came under my notice, because common decency forbids a recital of the horrible details. Much I have told has necessarily been of a personal character, which I would have evaded if I could, but I wanted to put on record for history's sake that which I knew to be true, and this I have done without malice or exaggeration as God is my judge.

Afterword

In recording his prisoner-of-war memoirs for his family, Ezra Ripple made several typewritten copies: two drafts remain on loose 8-inch by 13-inch sheets now brittle and brown-edged, and there are three professionally bound leather-covered copies, each with gaps in the text for insertion of the photographically reproduced drawings. As part of his commission to illustrate the work, James E. Taylor was also asked to provide a set of hand-colored projection slides for use in a YMCA lecture series based on the memoirs. For this purpose the original pen-and-ink drawings were reproduced on glass and then individually colored by the artist. These slides along with the Ripple family's hard-bound copy were inherited by my uncle, Ezra Hoyt Ripple Jr., and have since been donated to the Lackawanna Historical Society in Scranton, Pennsylvania, which also owns the second bound copy, originally given to Ezra Ripple's friend and business associate, W. L. Connell. The third bound copy, made for his sister, Mary Ripple Doster, was given by the Doster family to my eldest brother some years ago and is now in my possession along with both unbound drafts, one being a final clean copy and the other including notations for the lecture series.

Born too late to have known our grandfather at first hand, my cousins, my brothers, and I nonetheless felt that we knew him well. Hadn't we often been spirited into his home by our mother's and uncle's recollections and found it a far livelier place than our own? Even now their stories, grafted onto our own memories, are as vivid as when we first saw them through Mother's eyes. She had also gathered and passed on to us other, older memories from her parents

Mary Ripple and brother Ezra, likely around 1850

and grandparents. Some of them were stories her papa, Ezra Hoyt Ripple, had told his children while they, like us, had crowded close, enthralled by their visions of "olden times." There was, for instance, the story of his father's boyhood which had led to his own naming. When Silas Ripple's mother was widowed with a family of fourteen children, she had no option but to send her sons out into the world to support their sisters and herself. While the older boys took whatever employment they could find, the younger lads were sent to foster homes, where they earned their keep as unpaid servants. Silas's lot fell to a mean-spirited rural doctor who overworked and mistreated the boy. When an elder brother stopped at the doctor's house that first winter and found the little fellow gaunt and ill clad, he angrily broke the contract and brought him back home. Again Silas was sent out, but this time he was apprenticed to a kindly shoemaker, Ezra Hoyt, who soon became a surrogate father to him and for whom he later named his own son. When grown, however, Silas became not a shoemaker but a hotel keeper, and one of the duties of his son, Ezra, was the onerous job of force-feeding the geese to enlarge their livers for pâté de foie gras—a procedure so loathsome that he forbade the delicacy ever being served in his own home.

As one reads Ezra Ripple's memoirs of Andersonville and Florence prisons, a strong impression of the writer emerges—his sensitivity and compassion for his fellow men, his capacity to view soldiers of both sides with unbiased understanding, his devotion to justice coupled with his faith in a just and loving God, and his remarkable ability to balance the sordid scenes with touches of nobility and graceful notes of humor. His love of music, too, and his skill with a violin are an essential part of the story and of the man. All these qualities combine in an image of gentleness, strength, intelligence, and generosity which could scarcely be counterfeited and which are further confirmed by my mother's recollections. He was too transparently open hearted for grudge-holding, penny-pinching, or niggling deceptions. Guileless, emotionally up front, and of keen sensibility, he was, in fact, as subject to explosions of alarm, anger, and frustration as to bursts of compassionate generosity. This incendiary side of his temperament, contritely acknowledged in his calmer moods, was well known to family and friends; and thereby hung many a tale.

The marriage of Ezra Hoyt Ripple and Sarah Hewitt Hackett in 1874 produced five children in quick succession (the first being an early mortality) and they in turn generated a household in perpetual ferment. Sally, a bright and gifted schoolteacher, added her exuberance to Ez's wide-open disposition, creating a warm, welcoming home despite the Victorian strictures of the time. Their door was always open to those in need, and their house became a haven for assorted friends, relatives, and visiting clergymen of the Reformed Episcopal Church, the religious observances of which were far more numerous and extended than average. Deeply committed to the precepts of Christianity, Sally and Ez firmly believed in dogmatic guidelines for the young, and although church-related functions were liberally spread through the week, Sundays were completely given over to prayer, Scripture reading, meditation, and at least two church services. For the adults these activities were voluntary and rewarding, but not always so for the children. While Honnie, the eldest and most circumspect, found them a welcome exercise in pious dignity, to Ez Junior they were a challenge for misbehavior, to rebellious Jessie a hair shirt, and to little Sue one more game of follow-the-leader. It needed only a single restless child suffering from boredom, however, to unwind all the rest. For the Ripples were a high-strung family from the parents on down, emotionally risible and given to suppressed hysterics at inappropriate times.

This nervous house-of-cards syndrome was most memorable at the funeral of Sue, who died of tuberculosis at seventeen. She had been a merry, bright-eyed girl, the darling of the family, and watching her decline and death was a cruel ordeal for them all. As the funeral cortege proceeded to the cemetery with the immediate family together in a closed carriage, someone made a trivial remark. Later nobody could remember who it was or what was said, but it was a pinprick that burst the tension. Someone gulped, someone else choked, snorted, or gasped, and they all erupted in paroxysms of helpless laughter. The more they scolded each other and struggled for control, the farther out of control they spun until, on arrival at the grave site, they all emerged with handkerchiefs held to their faces, bodies racked by hysteria.

Ez's military background contributed to his insistence on discipline within his home. Since corporal punishment was the accepted means of correcting intransigent boys, Ez Junior had felt the sting of his father's horsewhip more than once—not savagely administered but sufficient to carry a clear message. The girls, though not exempt from punishment, were subject to less stringent measures. There was, for instance, the day when no one would admit to spilling ink on the carpet. Somebody, therefore, must be lying, and although the ink spill could perhaps be forgiven, the lie could not. Papa, examining them all for telltale stains, found none, but discovered that Jessie had

Ezra Hoyt Ripple, circa 1876

recently washed her hands. Accused, she hotly denied spilling the ink. Her hands were clean, she said, because she had been helping in the kitchen. Very well, then, she could go to her room until she was willing to tell the truth. She went, and stayed there until well into the next day, when Honnie tearfully confessed her guilt. Furious over her unjust treatment, Jessie refused to come downstairs or to speak to her father until he apologized—which he did most contritely, accompanying his words with a handsome piece of jewelry.

Although determined that his children should respect both sacred and secular authority, Ez was an affectionate parent who enjoyed bouncing the little ones on his knees and later, when they were bigger, taking them on excursions. One such treat was a trip to the circus with Jessie and Sue, which was more memorable for its misadventures than for the scheduled program. The show, as usual, was set up in a vacant field, using elephant power to haul animal cages and heavy equipment and to raise the big tent. Sue, her eyes everywhere but on her feet, started the day by stepping in an empty posthole not once but twice, jerking Papa off balance and triggering alarm signals throughout his nervous system. After an explosive "Thunderation!" or two he paid their admission and hustled the two girls up the wooden bleachers. Just as they were getting settled, however, his umbrella escaped him and went clattering through the slats to the turf some distance below. There was no way of retrieving it but to crawl through the open-backed benches and drop to the ground feet first. In the midst of this awkward maneuver his activity caught the eye of a roustabout who was prowling beneath the bleachers to spear trash with a sharp-pointed pole and to discourage gate crashers. "Hi, there!" the man shouted, prodding Ez's nether parts with his pole. "Think you can sneak in without paying, do you? We'll see about that!" The ensuing scene accompanied by Ez's bellows of rage was a bonus for the audience and an indelible memory for Jessie and Sue long after the circus acts had been forgotten.

Episodes of this sort were cherished by his children, not just from a simpleminded taste for buffoonery nor because they were typical of life with Papa. On the contrary, it was by contrast with Papa's normal persona that such scenes were startling and impressive. Ez's panic reflex resembled that of a splendid Thoroughbred horse shying at some incongruous object blown across its path. Similar outbursts of wild-eyed alarm were remembered too when his composure was jolted by some adverse and unpredictable happening. There was the time when, during a peaceful supper at home, a muted thump in the distance grew to a cumulative thudding, then a clattering, crashing, thundering avalanche of sound suggestive of a wing being torn off the house. Ez was galvanized but without a direction in which to launch his attack or defense. Suddenly the noise stopped as mysteriously as it had begun and everyone was sent running about the house in search of the wreckage. It was finally found to be in an enclosed staircase, where a boot, left in precarious balance on the top step, had made its descent, collecting assorted objects from successive steps until the whole mass had come to rest against the door at the bottom. The initial alarm was one thing. The aftershock of exasperation was another. Then there was the night when a fearful crash downstairs roused the household. It turned out that Ez, returning late from a meeting and not wanting to light a lamp, had barked his shin on a living room rocker, and in a wild surge of pain and fury had flung the offending chair out through the front window, which happened to be closed at the time. He was found rubbing his shin and breathing hard. "Ez Ripple!" cried Sally. "Aren't you ashamed of yourself?!" And, of course, he was. Then finally there was the evening when, on his way home from work with a pail of oysters, his toe caught on a loose board in the wooden sidewalk, spilling both him and the oysters galliwest. This time his adrenaline was not exhausted until he arrived at his own gate, having torn up each remaining board with his bare hands. Contrite, he ordered the whole sidewalk repaired the next day at his expense.

Sally and Ez were active in a wide range of civic and charitable organizations, but, unknown to the community, there were also many cases of private and personal duress in which they involved themselves. Their home, as before mentioned, was often a haven for family, friends, or even strangers with major or minor troubles. One of these was Hattie Featherman, a young girl who came seeking work as a housemaid. Impressed by her quiet, capable manner, Sally hired her and soon learned her story of rejection and despair. Turned away by her family because of an unwanted pregnancy, she had given birth in a women's shelter, where her baby had been put up for adoption. Now, without family, friends, or marketable skills, she was trying to earn a living as best she could. Convinced that the girl had untapped capabilities and deserved a better life than this, Sally enlisted Ez's help and together they arranged for Hattie's admission to a nursing school, where she excelled at her studies and was launched on a rewarding career culminating in her appointment as superintendent of nurses at a large city hospital. Years later, learning that she was terminally ill, the Ripples made room for her in their home, where, at her wish, she remained until her death and was buried in the

Ripples' cemetery lot. Not long afterward, Hattie's family showed up at the door. They had heard of her death and had come to demand their inheritance. On that occasion Sally's explosive response matched any performance Ez might have given, and the Featherman relatives beat a tactical retreat.

A problem similar to Hattie's reached Ez by a different route. A socially prominent friend and colleague confided in him that his unmarried daughter was pregnant and that already there were intolerable whispers and speculations among their acquaintances. What in the world could be done? Immediately Ez offered to inquire about "lying-in" homes in distant cities and to accompany the girl himself when an appropriate one could be found. As to the rumors, he would stop that: Since the Ripples' new baby was due to be christened in a few days, he promised that the child should be named for his friend's daughter as a public endorsement of her character. "That," said he, "will put a stop to any gossip in this town!" And so my mother, to her everlasting annoyance, was named Jessie instead of Elizabeth. As promised, Ez escorted the delinquent Jessie by train and taxi to the establishment of Mrs. Elida Swann in Chicago. When the girl was led away to her new quarters, Mrs. Swann drew herself up exceedingly straight and addressed Ez: "As for you, young man, I wonder you can still hold your head up after your ruination of this young woman!" And she continued to give him such a dressing-down as he had never received in his adult life. Throughout her righteous lecture he stood patiently, never attempting to defend himself, and when the tirade was over, he humbly departed. Once home, he said nothing about the interview with Mrs. Swann except to remark that she was an uncommonly fine woman of high moral principles. But when Jessie's parents later visited their daughter in her "confinement," Mrs. Swann ended her report with "I can assure you I gave that young rascal who brought her in a tongue-lashing he won't soon forget!" "Oh, Mrs. Swann," cried the mother, "how could you make such a dreadful mistake? That was our dear friend and benefactor, Ezra Ripple!" Mrs. Swann at once wrote to Ez, apologizing profusely, and Sally relished the story when she heard it. Thereafter a lasting friendship developed between them, and Elida Swann's picture remains today in the Ripple family album.

Ez's and Sally's efforts to lend a helping hand, however, were not always successful. Jack Barr is a case in point. He came to their attention through a local foundling home which they had actively supported for many years. Now in their upper fifties, the Ripples contested the report that Jack was a "bad seed," unsuitable for adoption, and decided to take him as their own foster child. Believing fervently that environment could overcome heredity, they offered a secure, loving home bolstered by religious and scholastic incentives to counterbalance the debits of "poor genes" and ill fortune. Unstable and insecure, Jack was prone to kleptomania and was more inclined toward falsehood than truth. Nevertheless, during the next two years of continued behavioral problems he developed an unqualified adoration for his foster parents. It was a heartbreak for them when Sally, unable to cope any longer, reluctantly agreed to return him. "But she would have succeeded if she'd been younger!" Jessie insisted. "They were both too old to handle it."

My grab bag of memories is seemingly bottomless, including but certainly not limited to events revolving around my grandfather. But the memories, one must remember, are inherited—heirlooms mulled over until they have gained the patina of familiar objects fondled in one's pocket. As hearsay they should be taken lightly by third parties, yet I doubt that they are any less true than our daily observations of people, places, and events in our lives. Although of a very different nature from Ezra Ripple's memoirs of the Andersonville and Florence prison camps, they may perhaps both confirm and extend one's understanding of the man himself as seen by other eyes at another period of his life and under very different circumstances. Both the stories told by him from his own remembrance and the later stories told of him by members of his family constitute a gift from one generation to another—an active touch of hands across the chasm of time past, time present, and time to come. Without such human bridges to inform, reassure, and comfort us, what use can any generation make of its muddling present and what offering give to the unwritten page?

Susan Ripple Richardson Hinkel
February 1995

Notes

Chapter 4

1. This was called "Stoneman's and McCook's Raid," which was part of Sherman's strategy during the Atlanta Campaign. The attempt to free the Union prisoners at Andersonville was to be tried only if parts of the raid had been successful. Stoneman instead moved directly on Andersonville, thus botching the overall plan and causing the capture of him and 700 of his men. Faust, ed., *Encyl. of the Civil War,* p.721.

2. Nelson Eveland enlisted on September 2, 1861, in Company A, 52d Pennsylvania, and was discharged on 21 June 1865. *History of the Pennsylvania Volunteers* (Vol. 3), p.63.

3. Bates's *History of the Pennsylvania Volunteers* (Vol. 3, page 86) erroneously lists Private David Davis as discharged on a Surgeon's Certificate on June 1, 1863. His child filed for a dependent's pension on February 20, 1865. Pension File Index of Union Veterans, National Archives.

4. This paragraph was copied from Ezra Ripple's handwritten insert found among the pages of his YMCA lecture manuscript. It evidently was an additional recollection after the "final" bound copies had been completed, and from both its context and physical location among the manuscript pages, it obviously was intended to be placed here.

5. Confederate prisoners were not as well off as Ripple suggested, but comparatively speaking, conditions in Confederate-Operated prisons were much worse than in Union-Operated prisons.

6. This was generally the term applied to Confederate prisoners who joined the Union army. Union prisoners who joined the ranks of the Confederacy were called "galvanized rebels."

7. James Barrett enlisted in Company A, 5th Georgia Infantry, on August 18, 1862, at Tyner, Tennessee, for the duration of the war. He subsequently was promoted to 2d lieutenant and transferred to Company C of the same regiment. This last record on file in his ser-

vice record indicates that he was on detached service of Nov./Dec. 1864 as Inspector of Military Prisons at Florence, S.C. Service Record. On September 6, 1910, his obituary appeared in the *New York Tribune:* "Lt. James Barrett . . . died in Augusta, Ga., yesterday, aged seventy years. Lieutenant Barrett fled to Germany to escape arrest following the war. He married abroad and returned to Augusta in 1870."

8. Private Josiah M. Wolfe, Company I, 143d Regiment, Pennsylvania Infantry, was captured at the Battle of the Wilderness on March 5, 1864. At the age of twenty-two, he enlisted on August 12, 1862, for three year's service. He was a farmer from Luzerne County, Pennsylvania, and had gray eyes, dark hair, and a dark complexion. He was paroled on 26 February 1865, and mustered out of service on June 12, 1865. Service Record.

9. Nineteen-year-old William Mills enlisted as a Private in Company A, 1st Wisconsin Infantry Regiment, on September 14, 1861, at Fondu Lac, Wisconsin. He was captured at the battle of Chickamauga on September 20, 1863. His POW record indicated that he also had been confined in Richmond and Danville, Virginia. Mills escaped from Wilmington, N.C. on February 22, 1865. He was mustered-out at Milwaukee on May 15, 1865. Service Record.

10. Andrew Jackson enlisted as a sergeant in Company I, 50th Pennsylvania Infantry, on September 25, 1861. He was wounded in action at the battle of Chantilly, Virginia, on September 1, 1862, and spent the next year and a half in the U.S. General Hospital in York, Pennsylvania. While he was still recuperating, he was assigned to the 79th New York Volunteers and then transferred back to the 50th Pennsylvania, which by now had become a "veteran volunteer" regiment. After returning to duty on April 15, 1864, the hapless Jackson was captured at Spotsylvania Court House, Virginia, on May 12, 1864. He was paroled at Charleston, S.C. on December 10, 1864, and was mustered-out five days later at the age of twenty-three. Service Record.

11. Ripple is referring either to the U.S. Sanitary Commission or the U.S. Christian Commission. Though similar in mission and philosophy, these organizations sometimes worked together but they were distinctly separate.

Chapter 5

12. There is no record of Collins Thompson in the 1st R.I. Artillery. There was, however, a "Thomas Collins" in Battery C, 1st R.I. Artillery. The muster roll for May/June, 1862 shows him as wounded and missing; he is later listed as "deserted" on August 1, 1862. The man to whom Ripple refers most likely is Collins V. Thompson, a musician in Company A, 16th Regiment Connecticut Infantry. He was captured at Plymouth, N.C. in April 1864. Service Record.

13. No record found.

14. The story of John January was well known among the ex-prisoners in the years following the war, and his story appeared in several published memoirs and histories. From his Service Record we know that Corporal John January enlisted in Company B, 14th Illinois Cavalry, in the fall of 1862, just as he was turning twenty-five. He was captured on Stoneman's and McCook's Raid during the Atlanta Campaign. Incarcerated first at Andersonville, then Charleston, and finally Florence, January was told by the Confederate surgeons at Florence that the gangrene he had contracted in his feet soon would kill him, and they refused to amputate. Wrote January, "believing that my life depended on the removal of my feet, I secured an old pocket knife . . . and cut through the decaying flesh and severed the tendons. The feet were unjointed leaving the bones protruding without a covering of flesh for five inches." January survived, was released at the end of the war, and lived for several more decades, minus his feet. Cited in John J. Fitzpatrick, ed., *The Andersonville Diary and Memoirs of Charles Hopkins* (Belle Grove Press: Kearny, N.J., 1988) pp.136-139.

15. Lieutenant Colonel John F. Iverson joined the Confederate army on May 11, 1861, as captain of Company I, 5th Georgia Infantry. He was promoted to lieutenant colonel on December 31, 1864. Iverson served on detached service from August 31, 1864, as the commandant of Florence Military Prison. He surrendered and was paroled at Greensboro, N.C. on May 1, 1865. Service Record.

16. Robert Burns's poem "Tam O'Shanter" was first published in 1791. See Geoffrey Tillotson, et al, ed., *Eighteenth-Century English Literature* (New York: Harcourt, Brace & World, 1969) pp.1472–1475.

17. R. Sidney Cheatham enlisted as a private in Company E, 5th Georgia Infantry, on May 10, 1861. Promoted to adjutant on June 4, 1862, he was on detached service to Florence from August 31, 1864. No further record of his military service exists. Service Record.

18. First Sergeant Peter Grohman enlisted in Company D, 16th Regiment of Connecticut Infantry, on July 19, 1862, at Hartford. Born in Germany, at the time of his enlistment he was thirty-three years old and was employed as a cigar maker. He fought at the battles of Antietam, Fredericksburg, and Suffolk, and was captured at Plymouth, N.C. on April 20, 1864. He mustered-out on June 12, 1865. Service Record.

19. No record found.

20. This was probably Second Lieutenant Calvin S. Kimball, Company C, 3rd Ohio Cavalry Regiment. He was twenty-eight years old when he reenlisted as a "veteran volunteer" in January 1864. In civilian life, he was an accountant. Kimball was captured on July 23, 1864, at Covington, Georgia. His POW records indicate that he escaped and reported to Union lines at Wilmington, North Carolina, on February 22, 1865. Service Record.

21. Iverson, Cheatham, and Barrett have been discussed in previous footnotes; of the rest of the men listed, none could be positively identified. There is record of a Private (not lieutenant) William Wallace, 5th Georgia Infantry, as being on detached service at Florence, December 31, 1864. Lillian Henderson, ed., *Roster of the Confederate Soldiers of Georgia, 1861-1865*, Volume 1 (Hopeville, Ga.: Longino & Porter, Inc., 1958) p.652.

Chapter 6

22. No record found.

23. Scant information was found concerning the wreck of the *S.S. General Lyon*, a merchant steamer under contract to the War Department, with the exception of a report in Series III, Volume 5 (pp.287–291) of the *Official Records*. This report was written on August 31, 1865, by Colonel George D. Wise, who was in charge of "Ocean and Lake Transportation" for the Union Army's Quartermaster Department. According to Wise, "only three vessels in the

service of the War Department" were lost at sea during the previous fiscal year (one of them being the *S.S. General Lyon)* The *"General Lyon* took fire and was burned." wrote Wise, "and the loss of life and property was not great" for the three vessels combined. This seems to contradict Ripple's belief that almost 700 exchanged prisoners died. This is not to be confused with the Sultana disaster, which was lost on the Mississippi River. On April 27, 1865, the sidewheeler Sultana left Vicksburg with 1,866 troops (mostly ex-prisoners) 85 crew members, 75 cabin passengers, more than 100 hogs, and 60 horses and mules. Grossly overloaded, the boilers exploded about 90 miles from Memphis, with a loss of almost three-fourths of the total on board. *Encyclopedia of the Civil War,* pp.731-732; Marvel, *Andersonville,* p.239.

24. Contrary to what Ripple believed, Stewart had not passed into "Fame's eternal camping ground." The twenty-two-year-old shipping clerk enlisted on February 17, 1864, as a corporal in Co. B, 97th New York Infantry, after transferring from the 83d New York Infantry. He was captured at the Weldon Railroad, near Petersburg, Virginia, on August 19, 1864. After being incarcerated at Belle Isle, he was sent to the prison at Salisbury, North Carolina. There is no record that Stewart ever was imprisoned at Florence. His mail probably was missent to Florence, which explains why Ripple believed it to be abandoned (and thus he thought Stewart had died). Stewart was released at Aiken's Landing, Virginia, on March 9, 1865. Service Record.

25. *Marvin Boget,* born in Greenfield, Michigan, stood five feet ten inches and had brown eyes, dark hair, and a light complexion. He was a twenty-two year-old farmer when he enlisted on August 13, 1862. Sergeant Boget was captured at the battle of Chickamauga on Sept. 20, 1863, and initially was confined at Richmond and Danville. He was paroled on March 1, 1865, and mustered-out on June 26, 1865. Service Record.

26. In 1904 Ripple applied for an increase to his federal pension. On the questionnaire sent to him by the Bureau of Pensions he was asked to describe any permanent marks on his body. Ripple answered that he had a "scar on upper muscle left arm and calf of left leg and calf of right leg bitten by dogs while trying to escape

from Florence, S.C. Military Prison, February 1865." Pension File, National Archives.

27. The article to which Ripple refers is T. H. Mann, "A Yankee in Andersonville," *Century Magazine,* July and August 1890, pp.447-461, 607-622.

28. The Patriotic Order of the Sons of America was founded in 1947 and is still in existence. It is a patriotic fraternal organization of American-born men "who place fealty to country above every other consideration." *Encyclopedia of Associations, 1994* (Detroit: Gale Research, Inc.), Vol. 1, p.2167.

List of Illustrations